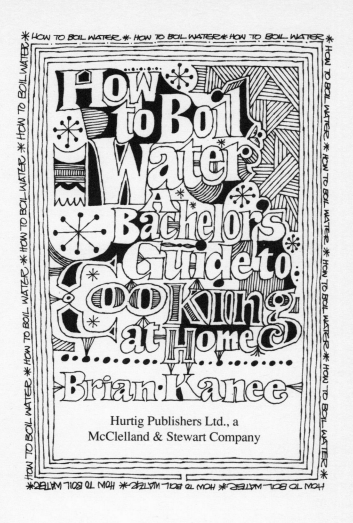

How to Boil Water
A Bachelor's Guide to Cooking at Home

Brian Kanee

Hurtig Publishers Ltd., a
McClelland & Stewart Company

Canadian Cataloguing in Publication Data

Kanee, Brian
How to boil water : a bachelor's guide to cooking at home

Includes index.
ISBN 0-88830-142-1

1. Cookery. 2. Menus. I. Title.

TX715.K36 1977 641.5 C78-005139-4

Hurtig Publishers Ltd.,
a McClelland & Stewart Company
481 University Avenue
Toronto, Ontario
M5G 2E9

Printed and bound in Canada

Contents

To friends and family . . . thanks for encouraging
a project talked about for years. To those special
people who kept me fired up and listened to me
rave when I hit a snag. To my secretary for typing
the thing. To LM for great editorial criticism.
To me for actually sitting down and doing the
work, researching, seeking, and accepting advice
and writing and rewriting until it was right.
To those who have sampled my cooking and
enjoyed it. In memory of my grandmother,
Rose Kanee, in whose kitchen this all started.

An Introduction to theWorld of Cooking

In an age where so much is mass - produced, it is often difficult to find outlets where individuals can express their personalities.

The art of cooking is one of the few remaining means of self expression. More people are discovering it as a way of providing valuable relief from the overdrive pace of the world.

This is especially so in the case of those who live on their own. Tired of crowded, smoky restaurants where good food and conversation is the exception rather than the rule, tired of one-way conversations over frozen dinners, they are turning to cooking as a fun hobby which they can practice to feed themselves and entertain their friends.

In concept the art of cooking attracts the bachelor, but in practice many are often at a loss as to how to bridge the gap between wanting to cook and actually knowing where to start. Perhaps he has prepared a meal or two. Perhaps the meals were not bad. But often the bachelor is robbed of the excitement of cooking through a lack of basic cooking know-how.

Turning to one of the thousands of cookbooks currently on the market, he is often overwhelmed and frightened away because there do not seem to be books devoted to the beginner, who often dines alone or with one other person, who hasn't the slightest knowledge of where to start and what to buy, and wants occasionally to entertain his friends on a modest scale.

At best the bachelor gets advice on dishes that are either beyond his capabilities as a beginner, take ten hours to prepare, or leave him with four pounds of unwanted leftovers.

Sometimes the desperate bachelor also seeks out books on the market that deal with budget meal preparation and finds that what he gets is food that saves him money but tastes uninteresting at the same time. So he is back where he started, interested but helpless.

True, there are a few scattered cookbooks dealing with the beginning cook and also a few on cooking for one or two, but none that combine the two with a slant to the bachelor, an individual who more often than not lives alone, likes good food, has limited time and money, and is tired of paying too much for good food in expensive restaurants or warming up someone else's frozen delights.

Most of the recipes in the early chapter of this book are tailored for this person, with complete cooking instructions and lists of ingredients. Most of the recipes take twenty minutes to an hour to prepare in menu form, taste good, cost relatively little, and can be made in limited space with limited equipment. Later chapters deal with more involved cooking for groups of people and for more formal gourmet meals in small, intimate gatherings.

In between is the guts of the book: things the bachelor will need to know before he attempts any cooking at all. Advice on what utensils he will need, how to stock his kitchen, tips and short cuts that can save him valuable time and money—all things that will change cooking from a means of survival to a lifetime hobby for him and his friends to enjoy.

There will be considerable effort devoted to making the reader feel at home and to involve him in what is going on in the book. It is written in his language and not in cooking jargon, so he can understand easily what he is expected to do each and every step of the way.

The book is meant as a guide only, whereby the bachelor can take his basic curiosity about cooking a step further and actually involve himself in meal preparation, creating his own delicious meals, because that is really what cooking is all about, cooking delicious things, using your imagination, and sharing your creations with other people.

Perhaps the bachelor I am talking about is you. This book will change your attitudes about cooking and, with a little effort, a lot of patience, and a sense of adventure, you will come up with meals that are just as tasty as those in the world's greatest restaurants. Of course the atmosphere cannot be duplicated, but you can come close, experimenting with your own table settings, mood music, and decor to create your own individual touch for dining. And you will find that in your own apartment or home you will unwind and relax. The evening will take care of itself.

Cooking for yourself, or dining in, can be fun. And let's face it, it is much less expensive than dining out. You will want to go to an expensive restaurant once in a while for a special occasion, but cooking for yourself will be far easier on your pocketbook.

And do not be afraid of mistakes; many great cooks have created meals that were far short of perfect. But the successes far outweigh the failures; remember that.

One other important thing to remember is that food has feelings. If you treat food well it will taste better. Spend a little extra time fussing over your meal preparaion and you will be amazed at the taste, not to mention the compliments from your guests.

For the most part, cooking is, and always should be, a fun thing, a hobby. Once you learn the basics, once you learn *How to Boil Water*, you are on your way to a lifetime of enjoyment.

But I am keeping you from the book. There is a lot to read and it is all fun; so let's get cooking!

·STOCKING·UP·

Okay cooking fans, time to stock up your pantry.

Stocking up is an art you should pay careful attention to early in your cooking career. Most of you probably impulse-buy, and although this may be fun it is very expensive and wasteful. The purpose of this chapter is to point out wasteful shopping habits and to shed a little light on some facts that can help you become better organized in the kitchen and have the right things on hand when you need them.

Buying on impulse is fine once in awhile, but over a long period of time it can dig into your savings. It really adds up. And you will have a lot of odds and ends that you will probably never use anyway, or by the time you do use them they are ready to be thrown out!

Sensible shopping is a fine science, but one easily learned. The first lesson you should learn is to make a list of what you need, total, monthly, and weekly. If you are not an organized person, then making lists and sticking to them, within reason, will eliminate expensive splurging. Of course now and then like anybody else, you are entitled to splurge, but try to keep it within reason!

A total list means an inventory of things you should have in the house or apartment at all times. The list allows you to build a basic stock of supplies. When you are out of something, you simply add to it. This is your monthly shopping list, and once it is completed you can shop weekly for other, more perishable things. After a couple of months, you will see how much time and money you can save! This way, shopping will become a pleasure again.

Of course, a well-stocked pantry means different things to different people, and a great deal depends on your budget and time, not to mention on how ambitious a cook you want to be. But most bachelors can get away with having only the following items in their cupboards and will still come up with most exciting meals, without having to rush to the market at the last minute:

Bay leaves

Cayenne pepper

Cinnamon

Dill weed

Ginger, powdered

Monosodium glutamate — known as MSG, it is often used in Chinese cooking, and is useful to soften meat of cheaper cuts.

Mint — great on lamb and vegetables

Paprika — hot!

Parsley — great as a garnish and as a seasoning

Peppercorns — grind them for your better dishes

Thyme — an all-round seasoning

Salt — a large box on hand at all times

White pepper — always necessary

Sugar — white and brown

Flour — unbleached white will do in most cases

Dry mustard

Whole pickling spice — not just good for pickling; also contains bay leaves, dill, and dried red peppers, all things you will need from time to time in your cooking adventures; so it saves spending money on each separately.

Garlic cloves

Garlic powder — a fresh garlic substitute

Garlic salt — a fresh garlic substitute, with salt

Cloves, whole

Instant chicken and beef boullion cubes — add instant body to soups, stews, and gravies

Chili powder — spicy and useful to pick up bland dishes

Curry powder — same, and often a novel change

Baking powder — for baking

Yeast — at least three packets if you plan to take baking seriously. They don't spoil if used within six months.

Dried chopped onion — great for last-minute additions to soups, stews, and gravies without messing your kitchen to dice one onion, also a great addition to chip-dips.

Extracts, vanilla, almond — extremely useful in baking and other cooking

Seasoning salt — a large container is wise as it can be used in all forms of cooking.

Sesame seed — use as a garnish in Chinese cooking

Shallots — hard to find but a delicious onion replacement

Worcestershire sauce — useful in all meat cookery

Soy sauce — buy two kinds, Japanese and Chinese, as each has its own respective and memorable taste. Again, many uses.

Tabasco sauce — a tangy addition to all meat cookery

Honey — buy liquid honey, and for a special treat try buckwheat honey. If possible, buy it directly from the beekeeper.

Maple syrup — for pancakes, but also perfect in many kinds of meat sauces, meats, and in baking

Oatmeal — either instant or regular, a snack that is also nourishing.

Cornstarch — for thickening sauces and gravies

Cocoa — both dark and light for baking

Baking chocolate — semi-sweet for most baking, but also get some bitter and some sweet as well, as you do not yet know which you will prefer.

Vinegar — essential in both regular white and red wine varieties

Ketchup — buy a large bottle as its uses are many, and keep it cold in the refrigerator.

Mayonnaise — for sandwiches and seafood salads

Miracle Whip — a slight variation on mayonnaise, but often preferred in the same dishes as it is sweeter

Prepared mustard — useful in meat cookery and sandwiches

Pickles — both sweet and kosher dills for appetizers

Cheese — keep an imported round variety pack in the refrigerator at all times, and also a sealed package of Mozzarella, Parmesan, and cheddar, for snacks and additions to salads, soups, and main course dishes. Unopened, the packages will keep for long periods of time.

HP Sauce — extremely useful in all meat cookery

Cooking oils, corn oil, peanut oil, vegetable oil, and olive oil — either one, two or three; buy all if you prefer variations in heaviness, peanut oil if you want an extremely light cooking oil.

Margarine — much more advisable than butter as it is substantially lower in cholesterol

Salad dressings — a matter of personal preference, but for plans to entertain you will need a thousand island, a French, an oil and vinegar, a Roquefort, and one diet dressing.

Mexican items — taco sauce, enchilada sauce, refried beans are all useful to have around for Mexican food lovers, together with some taco shells.

Canned prepared tomato sauces — at least three 5½-ounce cans

Canned prepared tomato paste — at least three 5½-ounce cans

Canned whole tomatoes — at least three 19-ounce cans

Canned fruits — a variety will do, according to your tastes, but try to stick to the natural juice varieties, as these will save you calories and taste just as good. Check the recipes ahead for a complete list.

Canned vegetables — three cans of mixed vegetables, two of mushrooms and two each of green beans, waxed yellow beans, kidney beans, peas, and carrots; for use in either vegetable dishes or stew. Check the recipes ahead for a complete list.

Canned soups — again according to taste, but one of each of your ten favourite varieties should do. Check the recipes ahead for a complete list.

Rice, pasta — one box converted rice, one box or package of spaghetti

Seafoods — two tins each of salmon, tuna, shrimp, sardines, oysters, anchovies, and crabmeat for salads and seafood dishes

Seasoned croutons — one box for garnishing salads or casseroles

Pie shells — one package prepared frozen pie shells for baking

Appetizers — one can each of green olives, black olives, mixed party nuts

Baking — one package each of walnuts, almonds, pecans, raisins, coconut, and figs

Three instant pudding mixes — depending on your tastes here

Frozen meats — for emergencies; and if you prefer to save time by buying, freezing, and defrosting as opposed to buying fresh each time you need a meat for cooking, then stock one whole chicken, two steaks, one boiling fowl (cut up), and two Cornish game hens.

Frozen fish — same applies here; you should buy one package of pickerel fillets, one rainbow trout, and one of cod.

Bread, cereal — keep at least two kinds of dried cereal, some frozen bread dough, a package each of cocktail crackers and graham crackers on hand for both snacks and additions to your dinner menus.

That should do it for your first shopping list. Bear in mind that you may have to cut back on this major list depending on your budget and space available for storage. All are not absolutely essential, but if you want to take cooking seriously try to get as many of the items as you can. It will save your running out at the last minute when a recipe calls for something on this list (and most will, at one time or another). Read ahead through the menus for an accurate list.

Now that the major list is out of the way, you can relax. Make weekly trips (again with a list) to your market for perishables. That means meat, vegetables, milk, and eggs. But plan again, and do not fall victim to the temptations of mass-merchandising that await you at your friendly neighbourhood supermarket!

It is a good idea to get to know one supermarket well, one you can come to trust for good bargains, good produce, and good meats. In fact get to know your butcher and store manager very well. They can do little things for you that you might not be able to do without benefit of their friendship. It is worth the effort to know your store and personnel in that store well.

UTENSILS

Plain or fancy, you are going to need to know how to equip your kitchen properly for the dishes you want to make. Do not rush out and buy imported utensils; at this stage you are not ready for them. Rely on your discount department store instead for most staple items. They sell for far less than the imported varieties and usually get you just as far in the kitchen.

Utensils can be divided into two basic types, essential and beyond essential. The essential things are fundamental to a small and growing kitchen such as yours; the beyond essential are things you should be giving some thought to if you want to take cooking seriously.

First of all, purchase cast-iron or aluminum saucepans (small, medium, large), and a frying pan (twelve to sixteen inches) in the same metal. For the best results, however, this may be one place to go out of the discount department store and purchase a copper-bottomed frying pan and saucepans, as they distribute heat more evenly and last considerably longer than aluminum. But cost here is the consideration, as the copper-bottomed items are considerably more expensive.

Now for knives: carbon steel knives are wonderful but expensive, and you have to maintain them carefully. Stainless steel knives, on the other hand, wear well, cut well, and are much easier to maintain. This is usually the kind for a beginner to get. You will need a twelve-inch chopping knife, plus other smaller knives, one a paring knife, the other general purpose.

Next purchase a kitchen utensil set, which generally consists of a two-pronged fork; a long, metal kitchen spoon; a long, slotted, metal kitchen spoon; a metal spatula; a smaller metal spatula; and perhaps a basting brush. This is absolutely essential and usually can be mounted on the wall beside the stove for easy use. Buying it as a set is often far less expensive than buying the utensils separately.

For measuring you will need a set of graduated plastic or metal measuring cups (one-quarter to one cup), or a pyrex measuring cup (two-cup capacity). Also for measuring, purchase a set of metal measuring spoons and a nest of graduated mixing bowls in either plastic or stainless steel.

Other assorted basic kitchen utensils include a grater with a variety of

16

grating edges, a funnel, a graduated metal mesh set of strainers, a rotary beater, a flour sifter, a better-quality plastic grip can opener (manual), a wooden spoon, a swivel-bladed paring knife, a pair of kitchen scissors, a teakettle, a teapot, an automatic coffeemaker or pyrex coffeemaker, a toaster, an electric frying pan, a pepper mill, a pastry brush, a rubber spatula, a basting syringe, a Dutch oven (three-quart, cast-iron ceramic) with handles, a graduated cannister set for flour and sugar and salt, a rolling pin, a metal whisk, two good pot holders and a good set of oven gloves or mitts, a full set of pyrex baking dishes, a roasting pan with rack, a metal roasting pan (either ceramic or aluminum disposable ones which are more reasonably priced), and *definitely*, a good pressure cooker.

Now onto things beyond the essential items, things necessary if you aspire to gourmet cooking.

First, buy an oven timer. Many bachelors have neither the time nor the interest to learn how to master the timing gadgets on their stoves, so this becomes necessary. With a timer you do not have to watch the clock and you can enjoy chatting with your guests while the food cooks.

Next, purchase a meat grinder. It ensures freshness in things like ground beef, as most store-bought ground beef is not that-day-fresh. Leftovers put through the grinder can be used in casseroles and meat sauces more easily.

A meat thermometer is a best bet to ensure that the meat you are cooking has been thoroughly cooked. Usually packaging directions on frozen, defrosted fowl advise a certain temperature for complete cooking, and you can read the thermometer when inserted in the fowl to see if you have, in fact, reached this desired temperature. This also saves your marring the appearance of the meat or poultry by hacking at it with a knife to see if it is done to perfection.

Muffin, cake, and pie tins are essential if you plan to start baking. Pyrex pie plates will do instead, and teflon coated muffin tins and pans, though slightly more expensive, are worth it in terms of ease of maintenance.

In advanced baking you will need a spring-form pan and a cast-aluminum tube pan as well. Both will satisfy you when you see the unique shapes of the finished baked products. Many supermarkets now carry these items as a matter of course, so look for them there.

An electric mixer and blender are handy, especially if you are a bachelor who does not enjoy hand-blending. Small electric mixers are on the market, some that include a set of graduating mixing bowls. You will find an electric blender is perfect for milkshakes and blending sauces, in addition to making superb mixed drinks and exotic punches. They can also be used for making soups and health food drinks out of fresh fruits.

Miscellaneous advanced essential utensils include an electric juice squeezer, a loaf pan, a two-quart decorative ovenproof casserole with lid, a soufflé dish, six earthenware ovenproof soup tureens, a fondue pot, a deep fat fryer, a Chinese wok for stir-frying Chinese dishes, a Mongolian hot-pot, a mallet and board for tenderizing meat, a meat cleaver, six custard cups, a copper-bottomed chafing dish, some good stainless steel metal skewers for trussing a stuffed fowl, a potato ricer, a garlic press, a vegetable slicer, a mortar and pestle for grinding spices and herbs, a colander for cooking and draining vegetables, a charlotte or ring mold, a crepe pan, and a waffle iron.

There are many other utensils on the market that might be valuable additions to your kitchen, but the ones discussed here should be enough to allow you to handle almost any meal, including gourmet meals, with ease.

Once you have progressed beyond the capabilities of this book, and you feel capable of trying dishes that demand very specialized utensils, take a trip to a reputable gourmet shop and seek out the equipment there. A shop that specializes in gourmet cookery will be able to offer you additional advice on these advanced utensils, and can often order things in that you may need in your meal preparation. But for now the items in this chapter should do nicely.

Tips & Short Cuts

III

What follows are some tips and short cuts that can develop your cooking sense and save you valuable time. After all, why spend your precious time on details when you need not do so?

On meal-stretching

Making food last past the first day is an art, but one that is so simple everyone should hear about it. Say, for instance, that you served a ten-pound roast turkey last evening to a group of friends, and after snacks, you are left with the poor fellow's skeleton, some meat scraps, and some stuffing. Why not do this: break the skeleton apart, put a two-quart saucepan on the stove and fill it with water halfway, and throw the little fellow in, bones, stuffing, scraps, and all! Then add whatever vegetable leftovers you may also have, such as broccoli, Brussels sprouts, lettuce, celery, and, if you have them, add two cans of mixed vegetables. Then boil the "stuffing" out of it, skimming off any scummy fat that rises to the surface, and letting it simmer for at least an hour. What remains is a turkey stew which can be eaten for dinner and usually serves four to six. The remainder of the stew can be either eaten the next day as a soup or frozen as a soup stock base for a future meal. You can get at least three meals out of a decent turkey and even more if enough scraps are left the first day to serve a hot turkey sandwich or a cold cut plate. For several days you have meals with virtually no fuss or preparation time, and cheaply too!

On pressure cooking

In a hurry? Late with the meal you said you were preparing for your guests? Only two hours until they come and you cannot do anything about it? If it is meat you are in luck if you have a pressure cooker. You have probably been or will be in this situation many times: people are coming and you have left everything for the last minute. Rely on your trusty pressure cooker to help you out of the jam. Simple to use, virtually messless, the pressure cooker is inexpensive to purchase and cuts cooking time *in half*. And you can get away with cooking less expensive cuts of beef this way. What you do is sear the meat lightly, then put it in the cooker and cook for as long as the cooker directions say. Usually a four-pound blade roast takes thirty-five minutes after the cooker starts to hiss. Then once the roast is done you put in sliced vegetables, including potatoes, and let them pressure cook in the gravy made by the roast. Then put everything into a cast-iron roasting pot and let it simmer gently in the oven for forty-five minutes or so. It "finishes" this way, and you can add a little cooking sherry to create a special flavour. This is an emergency recipe, but the pressure-cooked roast really does taste delightful and is always tender.

On cheese

Say you have just cut some cheese and you do not want the surface to dry out. Spread a little butter on it and it won't.

On potatoes

If you want baked potatoes quickly, speed up the baking time by parboiling them for five minutes and then bake in a 400 degree oven for forty minutes.

On Jello

If you want fast-setting Jello, add several ice cubes to one-half of the hot liquid. Setting time virtually halves.

On meat slicing

Slicing meat for sukiyaki or stroganoff? Put it in the freezer for one-half hour before slicing and it will firm up, making slicing easier.

On herbs and spices

Keep herbs and spices in alphabetical order for convenience.

On smells

To remove the fishy smell from fish, soak the fish in salted warm water for five to ten minutes.

On tomatoes

If you want easy-peeling tomatoes, dip them in boiling water for thirty seconds and then into cold water.

On burning

If broiled or grilled meats are burning, cover them with aluminum foil to cool them off. This also applies to overbrowned pastries.

On hard boiling

Perfect hard-boiled eggs can be made by bringing them to a boil, then lowering to simmer and cooking exactly fourteen minutes (well, fourteen and a half!)

On buns

Use frozen bread dough when making cinnamon buns in a hurry. The dough is sure to rise, is perfect every time, and saves messy hands and kitchens.

On onions

For a small amount of onion, cut deep crisscrosses over the cut surface and then slice. Keep the remainder fresh in plastic wrap.

On mustard

Mustard adds guts to cheese omelets. A teaspoonful will do.

On rust

Cast iron rusts. To prevent this, rub with cooking oil when not in use.

On stale bread

Bread gone stale is good for breadcrumbs; do not throw it out. Simply crumble it while still half stale and bake it on a cookie sheet for a couple of minutes, storing it in plastic bags for future use. Why buy commercial crumbs when you can make your own?

On garlic

Always, but always, keep several cloves of garlic on hand. They can be used in everything from soup to nuts.

On servings

If you are serving vegetables, plan on one-half cup per person or one one-pound-eleven-ounce can of same for six people.

22

If it is soup, then plan on one cup per person or three ten and one-half to eleven-ounce cans of same for six people.

Rice for six people would be one-half pound, based on approximately one-half cup cooked per person. Store any leftovers.

Serving coffee? You can get away with one-quarter pound for six people, based on a serving unit three-quarters of a cup per person. With milk, one-half gallon should serve six nicely. Meats take calculations. Beef chuck roast, for instance, would have you buying a three- to four-pound roast with the bone in for a four- to five-ounce serving per person. You may want more, and the leftovers could be used for days!

For ground beef recipes (some debate here) buy one-half pound per person, based on one-quarter pound patties. This means you should be buying three pounds of ground beef for six people, particularly if it is for a hamburger barbecue or chili.

Ham, baked and sliced, would have you buying a two- to three-pound ham for six people, based on servings of four to five ounces per person.

When buying chicken (again some debate) buy on the basis of one-half chicken per person, because some people are *chicken eaters*, and some are just chicken eaters. This means six people should demand three chickens. You will also want at least a four- to six-pound turkey for six people, as shrinkage and bones take up a great deal of the turkey's bulk.

One-half pound uncooked pasta should yield enough to feed six people well, based on a serving of three-quarters cup cooked per person. Perhaps your friends, if Italians, would be insulted at this paltry estimation.

One head of lettuce should do for six people for salads and one pound of onions for the same number. One pound of frozen green or wax beans for six, based on one-third cup per person, and one pound of frozen carrots for six on the same basis, as with whole kernel corn and peas, also frozen. Cut this in half with frozen French fried potatoes.

On starting a meal

When a recipe calls for certain things and you must start with others follow this guide: If it calls for five and one-half cups cooked fine noodles, you start with an eight-ounce package of fine noodles. One cup uncooked noodles equals one and three-quarters cups cooked. When it calls for four cups of sliced raw potatoes, start with four medium-sized potatoes. If it needs two and one-half cups sliced carrots, buy one pound of raw carrots; and four cups of shredded cabbage can be had from a small one pound cabbage. One medium-sized lemon will yield one teaspoon grated lemon rind and two tablespoons lemon juice (frequently called for in recipes). Two slices of fresh bread equals one cup soft bread crumbs. Six or seven large eggs yield one cup of egg whites, while you need a dozen large eggs for one cup of egg yolks.

On substitutions

What if you do not have what the recipe calls for? Then substitute as follows: For a clove of fresh garlic substitute a teaspoon garlic salt or one-eighth teaspoon garlic powder. One teaspoon freeze-dried chives will fill in nicely for one tablespoon finely chopped fresh chives. Use flour instead of cornstarch if you want, except double the measure. A cup of skim milk plus one teaspoon of butter or margarine fills in for one cup of homogenized milk. Seven tablespoons of vegetable shortening take the place of one cup (two sticks) of butter or margarine.

On measurements

1 tablespoon equals 3 teaspoons
2 tablespoons equals one fluid ounce or ⅛ cup
1 jigger equals 1½ ounces
¼ cup equals 4 tablespoons
⅓ cup equals 5 tablespoons plus 1 teaspoon
½ cup equals 8 tablespoons
1 cup doubles that
1 pint equals 2 cups
1 quart equals 4 cups
1 liter equals 4 cups plus 3⅓ tablespoons
1 pound equals 16 ounces

On can sizes

Portions are often confusing to bachelors in preparing meals, so an important tip to remember here is, a three and one-half to five-ounce can or jar will serve one person nicely, equalling a one-half cup serving. Therefore, an eight and one-half-ounce can or jar yields one cup and serves two people, a twelve-ounce can yields one and one-half cups and serves three people, a one-pound can or jar yields two cups and serves four people, a one pound thirteen ounce can or jar yields three and one-half cups and serves seven people, and a three pound two ounce can or jar yields approximately six cups and serves twelve people. In cooking for large groups of people, it is cheaper and more convenient to buy the large cans or jars.

On cooking vegetables

How long to boil vegetables until they are fully cooked often stumps the bachelor, so here is a brief tip on cooking times. Green or yellow beans, boiled whole, take fifteen to twenty minutes, but half that time when cut cross or lengthwise. Broccoli, after removing the tough lower stalks, takes ten to twelve minutes, while Brussels sprouts take ten minutes. Cabbage, green, takes five to eight minutes when finely shredded, and eight to twelve minutes when cut in chunks. Chinese cabbage takes less time, when finely shredded only four to five minutes, but red cabbage takes considerably longer, some fifteen to twenty-five minutes. Carrots, scraped or pared, and cut crosswise, take six to twenty minutes, while quartered take fifteen to twenty-five minutes. Whole carrots may take a full thirty minutes. Cauliflower, once you have removed the outer leaves and stalks, takes twelve to eighteen minutes whole, and eight to ten minutes if broken into small pieces. Celery takes eight to fifteen minutes, while medium onions take thirty minutes, or twenty minutes when they are small. Peas take about fifteen minutes fresh from the pod, while whole potatoes take thirty-five minutes, or twenty minutes when cut up. Zucchini takes fifteen to twenty minutes. While this is not a complete list, these are the vegetables you will most likely prefer in your cooking.

On volume

And did you know that many foods, when cooked, double in volume from their measurement before cooking? True. For instance, noodles, rice, and rolled oats all double in volume. Spaghetti quadruples, as does corn meal, while dried vegetables such as kidney, lima, navy beans, and green peas all yield double volume; so take this into account when cooking them. For desserts, remember that whipping cream also doubles in volume when fully whipped.

On timing your dishes

A very valuable knack to master is how to get all the dishes in one course finished cooking at the same time. This is a question frequently asked by most bachelors, who often find one thing done when others are not and as a consequence often overcook the former, causing the finished product to suffer. Well, do not despair. This problem is one that plagues not only the bachelor but the expert as well.

In meal planning keep in mind the number of stove burners you have available in relation to the stove-top cooking you want to do. Same goes for oven dishes. Do not plan more cooking than space available.

Also you have to allow for both preparation time and cooking time in your schedule. List all of your dishes in the menu, from soups, salads, main courses, appetizers, vegetables, sauces, through to dessert. Then allow preparation time for each and list that alongside the dish. Finally allow cooking time, and list that next alongside the dish. For instance broiling chicken takes five minutes to prepare, but thirty to forty minutes to cook, while soup from the can takes one minute to prepare, but ten minutes to cook. And with a salad, you may have ten minutes preparation, but no cooking time.

You have to allow for the oven to preheat, for the soup to boil, for the salad to chill once prepared. Often the first thing to prepare is the salad, well ahead of time. Then put it in the refrigerator, without dressing, to chill until it is needed. Then, preheat the oven, and while it is heating, set the table, open the can of soup and set it on the burner at ready, and, if you are baking French fries, peel potatoes, cut into chips and parboil for three to five minutes in boiling water. All this can be done while the oven preheats. Then put the chicken into the stove at broil, warm the soup, and serve. When the soup is finished, put the chips in the oven and turn the chicken. Twenty minutes later you have broiled chicken and browned chips, and the meal has gone off on time. Dessert, if any, can be done while the chicken is into its final twenty minutes, as most of the desserts in this book take only fifteen minutes to prepare.

On storage

Storage, how to store and for how long, can also be a problem for most people. Canned foods, unopened, have a long shelf life, provided they are stored in a cool place. The higher the temperature, the more they lose color and flavour. Once opened, they can be stored in the fridge for several days, but try to avoid storing in their original cans as the cans will impart a metallic taste.

Jams, jellies, and syrups can be stored in the refrigerator for long periods of time, but not for long at room temperature, while condiments, such as mustard, relish, and ketchup keep over long periods of time in the refrigerator. Shortenings and salad oil keep for long periods at room temperature, while breadstuffs and baked goods keep for much shorter periods. Bread crumbs should be stored in sealed jars, as should rice and cookies. Cereals can be stored in their original boxes, but prolonged storage is not advisable.

Dairy products should, of course, be kept cool in the refrigerator, but never for too long. Fresh produce also keeps for long periods of time, but it is wise to take it out of the wrappers and keep fairly dry in the refrigerator.

For potatoes in particular, and with onions, storage in a small box or bin under the sink or in a dark, cool, dry place is often favourable.

Meat storage is also important. Obviously, all meats should be kept cool in the refrigerator until used. For best results, beef roasts and steaks can be kept refrigerated for three to five days, ground beef and stew meat for two. With pork roast, two to three days storage is maximum, as with pork chops, spareribs, and sausage, but hams and bacon will keep considerably longer— seven days. Veal and lamb roasts will last five days, while veal and lamb chops keep two to three days. Chickens, whole or cut up, as well as turkeys, will last only two days. Most cooked meats, whether leftover ham, frankfurters, sliced luncheon meats, or bologna will keep for four days, but cooked chicken lasts only two days. Note that these are only approximate storage times. Your meats may last longer or shorter periods, depending on your refrigeration equipment.

On freezing

Knowing how to freeze your foods properly is important, whether raw
food or leftovers. Most meats, vegetables, fruits, soups, and desserts can be
safely frozen, but some fare better in the freezer for longer periods of time
than others. For instance, beef, lamb, and veal will last nine to twelve
months in the freezer at maximum, while ground beef lasts only three to
four months. Whole chickens will store up to twelve months without ill
effects, but cut up chickens last only six months and chicken livers three
months. Fish, cooked fish, and shellfish last three months, but fruits, fruit
juice concentrates, and most vegetables last between ten and twelve months.
Cooked casseroles can be stored for two to three months, as can soups and
most prepared main dishes. Desserts vary, as do breads and rolls, but a safe
bet for all would be three months at maximum. Be more careful, though,
with sandwiches and leftover cooked foods, which last only two to three
weeks before losing their taste and texture. Avoid storing salad type
vegetables in the freezer, such as lettuce, celery, and tomatoes, as they
drastically change their texture due to their high water content. This is
particularly evident in storing cooked chili and spaghetti sauce.

On defrosting

Meat takes about five hours a pound to thaw in the refrigerator, while at
room temperature, it is half that time. Shellfish take an hour per pound at
room temperature, while it is three times that in the refrigerator. For
poultry, take three hours at room temperature, but six to ten hours in the
fridge. Fish takes four hours at room temperature and double that in the
fridge. A best bet is to defrost most things overnight the day before they
will be used at room temperature, and then chill them in the refrigerator
until they are cooked.

On growing food and saving money

Saving money through grow-your-own foods is a valuable skill for the
bachelor to learn and can also be fun as a hobby. Depending on where he is
located as to climate, the energetic and enterprising bachelor can often grow
his own vegetables, fruits, and herbs quite inexpensively and with a minimum
of effort. In fact even when the outdoors no longer permits planting, the
addition of an ultraviolet lamp and some clay pots filled with earth can
provide the bachelor with a winter's growth of fresh herbs for his kitchen.
    Assuming that the bachelor lives in an apartment complex and has a
balcony, the least expensive method of growing vegetables, fruits, and herbs
is to invest in several (five to six will do) aluminum oven basters, some peat
moss (one large bag), and fifty pounds of earth (bagged and sterilized).
Mixing the earth and peat moss equally, dampening it, and filling the trays

with it entitles the bachelor to a chance for success as a gardener. With vermiculite under the earth as a drainage layer and holes punched in the bottoms of the pans, all the bachelor needs is an assortment of seeds and some sun.

The easiest vegetables to grow are carrots, peas, radishes, onions, green and yellow beans, and cherry tomatoes. These are things you will use constantly and can be stored for long periods once pulled. They also grow very easily in this temporary kind of environment. Fruits that can be easily grown are strawberries and raspberries. The same planting procedure goes here as for the vegetables. A little water every day and you should be eating fruit by the end of the growing season.

On herbs

The same advice goes for herbs, which take readily to this kind of planting environment, both indoors and out, while fruits and vegetables only respond to outdoor stimulation. Herbs, when grown fresh and properly dried and stored, are tasty and far less expensive to grow than to buy at your supermarket! The easiest to grow, as the song says, are parsley, sage, rosemary, and thyme, and are all frequently used herbs in your kitchen. Others such as sweet basil, oregano, and mint are also useful to grow and store. The use of herbs is determined by a recipe, but for you, an outline of the basic uses for the herbs mentioned here would be extremely useful.

Sweet basil can be used in all seafoods, most soups, salads, meats, poultry, stews, gravies, venison, game, fish, and vegetables.

Oregano can be used in soups, stews, borsch, gumbos, tomato seasonings, chowders, pork, veal, lamb, most vegetables and omelets, and Italian dishes.

Rosemary is used in soups, chowders, meats and vegetables, fish, poultry and game stuffings, and with turnips.

Sage can be used in soups, meats, fowl, fish, and vegetable dishes.

Mint is best used on lamb.

Thyme is used in soups, meats, chicken, or vegetables.

Another important tip in the use of herbs in cooking is the making of herb butters, which can enhance any meal. Using a full tablespoon of fresh herbs or two teaspoons of dried herbs to a pound of butter, first let the herbs stand in lemon juice before adding to the butter. Then mix the two together until well blended. Once prepared in this fashion, the herb butter is delicious as a spread on steaks or fish or to butter sandwiches or baste roast. Ideal here are parsley, chives, or marjoram.

And herbs are also used in a bouquet garni, a selection of fresh or dried herbs such as basil, marjoram, thyme, onion, or celery leaf, all tied in a small cheesecloth bag and immersed in soups, sauces, and gravies and removed before serving. A French invention, this use of herbs will enhance any dish in which it is used.

A final tip in the use of herbs is to remember that dried herbs are three to four times as strong as fresh, so use dried herbs much more sparingly in your cooking than fresh ones!

On cooking terms

Basting. Pouring or dripping a liquid over meat while it is cooking to keep it from drying out. You can use either the juice that has collected at the bottom of the pan, water, wine, or a mixture of all three. And always add a little soy sauce to any baste, as it usually adds something extra and browns the meat nicely at the same time.

Browning. For meat or poultry, browning is done on top of the stove in a skillet with a little fat, butter, or cooking oil. Meat is browned when it is a golden colour. Browning seals in the juices and makes the food look better; the oven will do the rest, cooking the dish right through. Browning potatoes or casseroles can be done in the oven, and is accomplished when a golden brown color is achieved.

Broiling. The same as grilling. Most modern stoves have a special setting for this technique. Note that in grilling or broiling, you must watch carefully, as the heat is extreme and comes from the top, so scorching can easily occur. If your broiled dish is scorching let it rest by covering the dish with aluminum foil, or move the grid to a lower setting in the oven.

Caramelizing. A method of cooking sugar over a low heat until it begins to melt and turns golden brown. Always stir it constantly while cooking and remove from heat after it browns but before it burns.

Creaming. If a recipe calls for cream it will say so, but when it asks you to cream something, it means to mix until it is of a fluffy creamy consistency, either with an electric mixer or by hand.

Devilling. Something you do by adding a spice or two, as in devilled eggs, when you scoop out the yolks from a hardboiled egg, add mayonnaise or Miracle Whip, mash, put it all back on the halved whites and top with paprika.

Dredging. You do not have to be an engineer to dredge. In cooking it means coating with flour. Usually dishes that call for dredging call for a seasoned coating of flour mixed with small pinches of salt and pepper.

Dusting. To coat lightly with flour, sugar, or icing sugar. Usually it is done after the dish is prepared, as for cakes, and serves to add visual appeal, but in the case of meats it is done before cooking and seals in the juices.

Filleting. To take the bones out of fish or poultry before cooking. A fillet, when called for in a recipe, is precut in this fashion.

Flambé. Setting food on fire using an alcohol-based ingredient, such as brandy or cognac. Care here must be taken to avoid using too much alcohol, as the flames can be harmful and quite suddenly go out of control.

Larding. To cover meat or fish with strips of fat, or to insert bits of fat into holes punched in meat with a special instrument called a larding needle. This is a good technique to remember in preparing roast beef, as it adds moisture.

Marinating. Soaking meat in a liquid mixture to flavour and tenderize the meat and/or game, and perhaps to take away any gamey flavour as well.

Pan broiling. Pan frying without using fat, or frying meat in a frying pan, but pouring off any accumulated fat. This form of cooking is really beneficial to your health, as the cholesterol count of the dish is substantially reduced.

Parboiling. Partially cooking a food in boiling water, thereby preparing or softening it up for easier cooking by another method. Particularly handy in making oven-browned potatoes in a hurry.

Paring. Cutting off the skins of vegetables and fruits. Sometimes the parings can be reinstituted into the dish afterwards, as in Moussaka.

Poaching. Cooking food at low heat (simmer) in a hot liquid, as in poaching eggs.

Purée. A technique for reducing food to a smooth sauce. This is usually accomplished by using an electric blender or a food mixer.

Reducing. A process whereby you boil a liquid down, intensifying its flavour. In this process you would, for example, reduce a beef stock to a beef jelly by boiling it down, or reducing it, gradually.

Rendering. Heating fat until it melts. You then save the liquid fat and throw away the solids.

Sautéing. Similar to browning, but for a longer period of time; cooking a food very gently in a skillet or frying pan on top of the stove in a small amount of fat or oil.

Thickening. Adding ingredients to a mixture to change its consistency from a thin liquid to one you can use in sauces, gravies, or soups. Some people use flour but others prefer cornstarch.

Trussing. Does not mean making a prisoner out of something! In cooking it simply means to tie the legs and wings of poultry close to the body cavity with string. This is done prior to cooking.

On how to make coffee

This knowledge is fundamental to the lives of most people and yet is something few know how to do properly. Coffee is the lifeblood of most bachelors, waking them up, sobering them up, and it is the perfect excuse for inviting someone up to your apartment. It complements any meal, gourmet

30

or otherwise, and is a perfect after-dinner treat served laced with fine liqueurs. It can even perk up tropical plants!

First, always remember that good coffee is clean coffee; so scrub the coffee pot well after each use, washing well with soap and water and rinsing carefully. Then proceed, using three-quarters cup of water with each measure of coffee, whether you have a drip, percolator, filter, or whatever. Add a pinch of salt to each pot and start with very cold water.

Grind coffee as you need it, using one of the relatively inexpensive coffee grinders available on the market (preferably electric), and keep your coffee beans in the refrigerator at all times for maximum freshness. Both things assure fresh, tasty coffee. Purchase two kinds of coffee from the super-market, caffeinated and decaffeinated. Some guests prefer decaffeinated, and you might, too, depending on whether or not you want to stay awake, as the decaffeinated variety will let you sleep. Instant coffee, while frowned on by most coffee purists, is a welcome addition to your kitchen as an additive to many dishes for flavouring, as in Chocolate Mousse.

Another useful thing to note about coffee is that the grinds are perhaps the greatest natural deodorizer known to man. Toss them into your garbage, and presto, no smell for days.

All about eggs

Another question frequently asked by many bachelors is how to prepare an egg. Well, eggs take watching, and care must be taken not to overcook them as they rapidly stiffen up. Begin with cold water when hard-boiling. This will allow the eggs to warm up as the water boils and avoid cracking and leakage. Barely cover the eggs with water in a small saucepan, bring to a boil, and then turn the heat down to simmer, cooking for four minutes if you want them soft-boiled, and fifteen for hard-boiled.

Poached eggs are another source of complaint for bachelors, so here is a tip on them. Put an inch of water in the bottom of a skillet and let it simmer gently. Add a tiny bit of vinegar to the water to keep the whites together and firm. Then, break the eggs, one by one, into a saucer, taking care not to break the yolks. Slide them into the water, again gently. When the whites have set, they are done and can be taken out with a slotted spoon and are drained of all water before serving.

If a recipe asks you to beat the yolks and whites separately, make sure that no yolks get into the whites. If this happens, you will never get a stiff white mixture. Separating an egg is easy if you remember to crack the shell over a small dish and tip the yolk back and forth between shell halves while the white runs out into the dish.

On to greater things

Still on basics, now is the time for a very simplified definition of what cooking really is. You will not find one simpler than this: cooking is taking raw food, clothing it in liquid and/or seasonings, and making it hot. It is taking the main dish to be served hot, usually meat or fowl, placing it in a pan, and adding things that will complement it's flavour, such as onions, green peppers, and mushrooms. Sometimes a liquid is poured over it to give it moisture and prevent it from drying out in cooking, and seasonings are added. It is then made hot by slow-cooking it in a pan or in the oven, and it is served hot. And you soon realize that, by adding a liquid such as red wine to a main dish such as chicken, you have unwittingly created a French classic, Coq au Vin.

Basically, cooking is really that simple, and the trick is to vary the additions (liquids, spices, heat) to the main dish. Add pineapple and honey to chicken, for instance, and it is sweet. But add soy sauce and broil and it is crisp. Adding different wines gives different flavours to dishes, as do fruit juices, so try them all if you can for varied effects.

One important thing to remember here is that taste is a personal thing. Do not let yourself be limited by restrictions such as one teaspoon, one-quarter cup, etc. Let yourself go; add a taste of this, a pinch of that, and a handful of whatever you think will go down. It's your kitchen, and you should be the one making the decisions, not a book.

The really big thing in cooking is seasoning. It can be the difference between liking or hating what you eat. By seasoning a dish, you can transform it from something bland into something tasty. But again a word of caution here not to overseason, as that can do as much damage to a dish as not seasoning at all!

On meat, fowl, and fish

Do not buy cheap cuts if you can avoid it, because they will disappoint you in most cases. As has been said before, make friends with your butcher and ask him to give you the best cuts personally. It will make the difference in what you finally prepare, whether it is a stew or a steak.

Chickens are a best bet when they are purchased fresh, but if this proves difficult, buy the best available grade frozen from a reputable supermarket. Of course, the best of all for both taste and quality is a country-raised bird that has been corn fed; so if you have any contacts in the country on a farm make use of them.

Fish is best fresh if you can buy it, but failing that, most supermarkets carry good selections of frozen fish. The taste, of course, is far superior in the fresh varieties. Do not let the smell of fresh fish drive you away. Once prepared, the taste of fresh fish is delicious. When buying fresh, look for bright bulging eyes, shiny scales, and red gills. Press the flesh and see if it is firm and plump. Try to buy it the same day you plan to use it as fresh fish quickly goes bad.

Shellfish, also, are best when purchased fresh, but adequate frozen. Canned, they lose a great deal of their texture and taste, but again this will have to do in a pinch if fresh or frozen are unavailable.

On vegetables

Vegetables are an important part of any menu and quite nutritious if cooked correctly. You should always try to buy your vegetables fresh whenever possible, and when cooking try never to leave them in the liquid they are cooking in for very long. Frozen vegetables are not bad, but canned are the worst as they lose again in taste and texture.

For the best bets in fresh vegetables, seek out a Chinese grocery store. This is so because the Chinese take great care in preparing the vegetables which comprise a large portion of their meal dishes and demand the very highest in freshness.

On leftovers

All right, now what to do about leftovers? The recipes that follow have been carefully prepared so that leftovers will be kept to an absolute minimum. Often what has been served one day will leave leftovers which can be used in another day's menus, as you will see. But even with careful planning, you may still find yourself with small quantities of leftovers and are no doubt wondering what to do with them before they spoil.

Usually the small quantities of leftovers are not enough for a full portion. So they sit around in your refrigerator, waiting to be used, but they seldom ever are, and are finally dumped unceremoniously in the garbage can. Much depends on your personal preferences. You may not like to eat a particular food once it has been cooked and has become a leftover. That choice is yours. But the following information should serve as a guide for your use of leftovers, dealing with the foods most likely to be left over in the course of normal mealtime consumption. They are in alphabetical order for your reading convenience.

Apples, cut up, last for a week when wrapped in plastic wrap and stored in the refrigerator. They may later be used in a fruit salad, or to flavour broiled meats such as pork chops.

Bread keeps for a week when wrapped and stored in the refrigerator in plastic wrap. Even better, freeze it; it lasts up to two months. Let it dry out and you can use it to make breadcrumbs. Stale bread makes good croutons.

Carrots, when stored in your refrigerator crisper drawer, can last up to a month, while celery will last ten days. Both may be used in menus such as stews, Chinese food, salads, or cooked in boiling, salted water as a hot vegetable.

Cheeses, cheddar, process, or other hard cheeses, last over a month if tightly wrapped in plastic wrap and stored in the refrigerator. They can be used in almost everything, from soups, salads, sauces, with fresh fruit, or just as a nourishing snack.

Chicken, cooked, lasts only a week in the refrigerator when wrapped in plastic wrap. During that week, it can be diced for use in Chinese food, cut up for a cold salad, or just eaten as is, cold.

Chicken livers do not last very long, only one day, but if served as a hot meal they can double as a cold hors d'oeuvre the next day if you have guests.

Coffee when frozen in ice cube trays keeps iced coffee cold, with an added touch. Also, the coffee grounds help deodorize garbage. Coffee may be used in desserts and dessert sauces.

Fish, cooked, lasts one day, and may be served cold on the second day in seafood salad, or seafood cocktail appetizer with chili sauce.

Ham and other cold meats, when tightly wrapped in plastic wrap, will keep for between one to two weeks, and are ideal for cold salads, sandwiches, or cut up into strips or cubes for addition to omelettes.

Lemons, cut, are perfect for squeezing into salad dressings, over fish, into pie fillings, over broiled meats before cooking.

Lettuce or other salad greens will keep for up to a week when stored in the crisper bin in your refrigerator in plastic wrap or the bag they came in. Use as needed, or as a nonfattening late night snack.

Onions, cut, last up to three weeks wrapped in plastic wrap in the refrigerator. Again, use as needed; fry with meats, use cold in salads, or as a flavour for vegetables.

Onions, whole, last for up to a month stored in a bin in their original bag. Take care not to allow them to become moist or they will soon rot.

Potatoes, raw, may be stored as whole onions and used as needed. Cooked, they will last a couple of days at best stored in plastic in the refrigerator.

Rice, cooked, lasts for three days in the refrigerator, and may be used reheated and fried, as Chinese rice, or in rice puddings as a dessert when cream and sugar are added.

Soups, when covered and stored in the refrigerator, can last up to a week, but it is a good idea to incorporate them into sauces and gravies as soon as possible.

Tomatoes, cut, will keep for a week in the refrigerator, wrapped in plastic. They are perfect to combine with other vegetables, rice, or add to a sauce or gravy.

Tomato paste, on the other hand, will last up to ten days in the refrigerator, covered tightly and stored in its original can. But to make it last much longer, for several months if necessary, freeze it instead. Use it in soups, sauces, and gravies.

Vegetables, cooked, last up to five days stored in a covered dish in their own liquid in the refrigerator. Depending on your upcoming menus, these vegetables are the perfect addition to soups, stews, gravies, and sauces.

Leftover wine can be used in sauces and gravies. It keeps for long periods of time, although it is advisable (many may disagree) to keep it chilled in the refrigerator to preserve its flavour. (The use of wine as an addition to any of the menus here is, of course, up to you. See Chapter VIII.)

Leftovers, if you have a little extra time, can be used to make great soups. Start with a two-gallon container, a gallon of water, salt, and heat, and add your leftovers, such as vegetables and meats. Even leftover wines can add excitement to a soup made from leftovers. Bring to a boil and serve hot, either strained or with the leftovers right in the bowl!

On mistakes

Another rule of thumb: do not be afraid of the mistakes you have made, because they can be disguised very easily. Of course, it would have been better to watch what you were doing more carefully in the first place, but, failing that, there are some things you can do to undo what horrors you have wrought!

Say you drown a dish with too much liquid. When this happens you can give the dish artificial respiration by cooking it a little longer. Not enough liquid, on the other hand, calls for liquid additions.

If it is too sweet, add lemon or salt or both. If it is too tart, add sugar. Too salty, add a potato and it will right itself. Too spicy, and again sugar will bring it back to life.

On rice

This is a special help to any cook and should be given careful attention by you bachelors. Simply by adding one cup of dry rice to two quarts of boiling salted water, covering, and letting boil at simmer for twenty minutes, you have a versatile food just waiting for imaginative additions. You can seldom fail with rice. If it is too firm, just add a little water and cook another five minutes. If overdone, rinse it in cold water. Once cooked, you can do millions of things with it. Add mushrooms, peas, cheese sauce, meat gravy, spices, curry, onions, fruits—in fact anything! And it can be served hot, cold, as a main course, a side dish, a salad, or a dessert. Investigate rice beyond this book. It may save many a meal for you.

More on portions

A simple rule of thumb in cooking meats is to plan on one-third pound per person. With chicken, try one pound per person, or one-half chicken, because most of the fowl's weight is in bones. The same goes for duck and turkey. And besides it is better to over-buy meat and fowl portions as the leftovers can serve you well for several days either cold, hot, in soups, or in stews, by simply adding other ingredients.

On nutrition and meal balance

Proteins, fats, carbohydrates—three categories of food the bachelor needs every day to stay alive and healthy. For the average bachelor, a favourable daily intake would be 12-20 percent protein, 50-60 percent carbohydrates, and 30-35 percent fats.

In other words, you will need some balance in your meals in order to eat nutritiously and this takes planning. If you overdo your carbohydrates and fats, you will simply gain weight in most cases. That you don't need!

So some attention should be given to planning your meals in terms of balancing essential food intake. As most of you are away from home for the morning and noontime meals, these will be dealt with only on the surface, outlining instead what you will need over the whole day, and leaving the planning to you personally. How you distribute the foods recommended over three meals is really up to you, but the evening meal is given most attention as to balance. Try to watch what you eat for the two other meals; avoid the heavy noontime meals so frequently consumed by the modern bachelor-businessman today.

One essential thing to remember, is not to skip a meal unless it is beyond your control. And try to avoid between meal snacks except for fresh fruits or fruit juices or the occasional glass of milk. Third, if you take tea or coffee try to avoid cream and limit your sugar intake. Doing this, you will find that you will start avoiding the midmorning letdown that frequently plagues the heavy coffee or tea drinkers. This will prove itself in better work concentration.

By serving foods from each of the four basic groups (1) milk, cheese, ice cream; (2) meat, poultry, fish, eggs, dry beans and peas, nuts; (3) grain products; (4) vegetables and fruits, you will be sure to maintain nutritional balance in your meal planning.

On a daily basis, you should try to have one pint of milk; one or more servings of meat, fish, and poultry (including liver); one egg; a leafy green or yellow vegetable and one potato; a half cup of citrus fruit or one cup of tomato juice; plus other fruits, either raw or cooked; three servings of breads and/or cereals; and two tablespoons of butter or margarine, preferably the latter to reduce cholesterol intake. (If you find it hard to maintain such a plan, supplement your food intake with a multi-vitamin to insure nutritional balance.)

And if you are asking what each of the above recommended servings includes, pay attention to the following: milk includes fluid, whole, evaporated, skim, buttermilk, cheese, and ice cream. If you prefer, a one-inch cube of cheese will replace a half cup of milk, and a half cup of cottage cheese will replace one-third cup milk. Of course, ice cream is different because of its high caloric value, so try only one scoop per cup of milk. The bread group includes breads, cereals, corn meal, crackers, flour, grits, macaroni, spaghetti, noodles, rice, quick breads, and other baked products.

So to plan a meal properly, take the above information on nutrition into consideration. Try to select a main dish from the meat or fowl category, add a bread or cereal product to complement it, then a hot or cold vegetable, a fruit or salad, and top it off with a simple, relatively sugar-free dessert. It's as simple as that.

And to make nutrition and meal planning even more enjoyable, vary the shape and color in the dishes you are serving. All foods can be prepared in a variety of ways that make eating not only nutritious but exciting. For example, rice or potatoes boiled, baked, fried, served hot or cold, spiced or with a gravy—in any fashion—they offer endless color and taste in their nutritional potential. The same goes for any other course on the menu!

You have now had enough tips and short cuts to excite you and prepare you for the world of cooking. Perhaps you are now ready to read on to discover how to change cooking from a means to an end, survival, to an end in itself, an enjoyable lifetime hobby. With the help of the next few chapters in the book, you may begin to find mealtime an event worth experiencing yourself and something to share with your friends.

Cooking for One or Two:
30 • Complete, Easy Menus

IV

After learning what to buy in the way of kitchen utensils, how to stock your kitchen, tips and short cuts to success as a cook, and how important nutrition is, the bachelor is ready to tackle his next big lesson: cooking for himself or for one other person.

Most bachelors find this to be the greatest difficulty to overcome: how to cook for one or two without buying things that will be wasted. They want to know how to cook complete meals quickly and simply, meals that will taste good, meals that are a welcome change from their usual diet of TV dinners, a can of beans, or grabbing a quick hamburger at their local drive-in restaurant.

This chapter is devoted especially to them and to cooking for one or two. In a nutshell, the chapter tells the bachelor what he will need, the length of time each complete meal takes, and what to do with the leftovers. There are thirty menus in all, one for every day of the month, all nutritious and tasty evening meals. The meals are flexible; the dessert from menu ten can serve just as well as a dessert for menu twenty-six. Great care has been taken to incorporate any leftovers into succeeding menus in the chapter.

What you will need for each individual menu will be listed under Ingredients. Many of the things will already be a part of your kitchen supplies, if you have acted on the suggestions in the chapter on stocking up. The remaining items will have to be purchased as needed. Bear in mind that some items will have to be bought, frozen, a day in advance of preparation and defrosted for the next day's recipe. These items will be listed in a reminder note at the bottom of the recipe if they are needed for the next day's menu, so look for them.

As well, bachelors should take note of the fact that the chapter basically outlines portions for two people. If you are only cooking for yourself, cut the portions in half (unless, of course, you have a large appetite).

And when cans of food are talked about, bear in mind that a three and one-half to five-ounce can usually is enough to serve one person, while an eight-ounce can will serve two nicely. With soups suggested in the menus, however, an eight-ounce can is usually all that's available, so leftovers may have to be used as snacks, or incorporated into upcoming menus in the chapter.

In all, this is really an essential chapter for the bachelor, and will start him on the road to survival on his own as a cook. Once he can handle the meals in this chapter, he will be ready to go on to cooking for crowds, entertaining, and gourmet cooking, all to be dealt with in this book. But before he can handle these skills, he must be able to feed himself and learn the basic art of cooking. Read carefully, and good luck, bachelors!

Tomato Juice
Seafood Mix
Bean Sprout Salad
Fresh Fruit

Approximate preparation and cooking time: 15 minutes

Ingredients:

1 3½-5-ounce can tuna
1 3½-5-ounce can salmon
1 small head fresh cauliflower
8 ounces fresh beansprouts, or
   canned
4 ounces (approx.) fresh
   mushrooms

1 medium green pepper
1 small can tomato juice
Fresh fruit
Cheddar cheese
Melba toast or RyKrisp
1 bottle prepared oil and vinegar
   dressing

Preparation and cooking steps:

1. *Bean Sprout Salad:* First, slice mushrooms thinly, break cauliflower into pieces, and cut pepper into strips after removing the seeds. Toss vegetables in oil and vinegar dressing in a large bowl. Set in refrigerator to chill until dinner is served.

2. *Seafood Mix:* Draining of all liquid from each can, empty cans of salmon and tuna onto centre of serving plate. Arrange salad around tuna and salmon on serving plate and grate cheddar cheese over the mixture. Serve from the serving plate onto individual dishes with fresh fruit and melba toast or Ry-Krisp as side dressings. Chilled tomato juice is an ideal beverage, perhaps with a touch of Tabasco sauce.

2

Apple Juice
Ham and Cheese Omelette
Tomatoes Zucchini
Cherry Sherbet

Approximate preparation and cooking time: 35 minutes

Ingredients:

1 small can apple juice
4 medium eggs
1 package sliced ham
1 small fresh zucchini
1 small can tomato paste

4 ounces grated cheddar cheese
1 medium onion
Salt and pepper
Margarine

Preparation and cooking steps:

1. *Tomatoes Zucchini:* Thinly slice the zucchini as you would a cucumber and dice the onion. In an electric frying pan or small skillet, fry the sliced zucchini and onion in margarine over medium heat, adding tomato paste and four ounces of water when onions turn golden, in approximately ten minutes. Drain mixture into small serving dish and keep warm in oven.

2. *Ham and Cheese Omelette:* Beat four eggs in large bowl and season to taste. Chop ham into rough pieces, and add to beaten eggs. Grate in cheddar cheese. Melt margarine in frying pan over medium heat, and pour in eggs. Lift omelette around edges to allow uncooked eggs to flow underneath. Cover and cook for approximately five minutes, uncover, fold omelette in half, and place onto serving dish. Spoon hot zucchini mixture over the omelette and serve directly. Apple juice, the beverage in this menu, can be served as needed, and cherry sherbet, the dessert, is available at your supermarket.

Note: Reminder to remove frozen fillets from freezer, or purchase in today's supermarket trip, so that they can thaw for tomorrow's meal.

3

Clamato Juice
Baked Fish with Cheese
Mixed Vegetables
Tangerine Ice Cream

Approximate preparation and cooking time: 40 minutes

Ingredients:

1 16-ounce package frozen
pickerel fillets
1 8-ounce can mixed vegetables
4 slices processed cheese (sharp)
1 small can Clamato juice
4 ounces flour

Salt, pepper, paprika
1 can orange sections or 6
tangerines (fresh)
Vanilla ice cream
1 fresh lemon or lemon juice
concentrate

Preparation and cooking steps:

1. Preheat oven to 350 degrees.

2. *Vegetables:* Remove mixed vegetables from tin and heat over medium heat in small saucepan.

3. *Fish:* Lightly flour and season fish fillets. Brown them quickly in two tablespoons of oil on both sides in skillet or electric frying pan. Transfer to baking dish, sprinkling lightly with paprika and the juice of one lemon, and place in oven for fifteen minutes, on top oven grid. Then remove and place cheese on the fish sections and bake another five minutes or until the cheese melts and begins to bubble.

4. *Tangerine Ice Cream:* While the fish bakes, squeeze juice from oranges and blend it either by hand or with a blender with a pint of vanilla ice cream. Refreeze until ready to serve as dessert.

Note: Purchase or defrost one and one-half pound ground beef for tomorrow's recipe. Reserve a half pound for Menu 5.

4

Cream of Tomato Soup
Stuffed Green Peppers
Spanish Rice
Honeyed Pineapple Slices

Approximate preparation and cooking time: 1 hour

Ingredients:

1 can cream of tomato soup
2 green peppers, medium
1 cup white rice
2 medium onions
Salt, pepper, chili powder, sugar,
    ground cloves, bay leaf

1 can whole tomatoes (1 lb. 12 oz.)
1 small can pimentos
4 ounces honey
1 can unsweetened pineapple slices
1 pound ground beef

Preparation and cooking steps:

1. Preheat oven to 350 degrees.

2. *Boiled Rice:* Bring two cups salted water to a boil, add rice, and cook twenty minutes over low setting, covering tightly with lid.

3. *Stuffed Green Peppers:* Remove centre and seeds from peppers by cutting a hole in the top of each pepper and scraping the inside, leaving the bottom intact. Chop one onion and pimento coarsely, draining all liquid from pimento first. Then fry the ground beef over medium heat in an electric frying pan or saucepan, adding chopped onion, pimento, chili powder, salt and pepper to taste, until the onions begin to glaze. Save the fat from frying. Press the ground beef mixture, once cooked, into the green peppers, place the peppers on a baking sheet and bake in the oven for fifteen to twenty minutes.

4. *Spanish Rice:* Fry the second onion, diced, in leftover fat from beef until tender. Add the can of whole tomatoes to the onions with a pinch of sugar, some salt, a bay leaf, and some ground cloves. Stir in the rice you have already cooked and set aside, and simmer for twenty minutes. Serve with the green peppers hot from the oven.

5. *Soup:* Open can of soup, heat in saucepan, and serve.

6. *Pineapple:* Open a can of pineapple slices, drain the juice and save in the refrigerator. Place four slices on a cookie sheet, cover each with two tablespoons of honey, and bake in still-hot oven until honey bubbles and slices begin to turn a golden brown. Serve at once.

Little Caesar Salad
Spaghetti and Meat Sauce
Spumoni Ice Cream
Espresso

Approximate preparation and cooking time: 30 minutes

Ingredients:

1 5½-ounce can prepared spaghetti
   sauce
½ pound ground beef
1 package thin spaghetti (No. 9)
1 pint spumoni ice cream
1 can sliced mushroom pieces
1 jar instant espresso
Garlic, oregano, salt, parmesan
   cheese, salt, pepper

1 head romaine lettuce
1 jar anchovy paste or 1 can
   anchovies, crushed
1 lemon
1 package prepared croutons
1 raw egg
Olive oil

Preparation and cooking steps:

1. *Spaghetti:* Heat can or jar of prepared tomato sauce in large saucepan or electric frying pan, add garlic clove (crushed), oregano, salt, pepper, ground beef, mushrooms, and let simmer, stirring occasionally.

2. *Pasta:* While sauce simmers, add one-half of the small package of spaghetti and cook in two quarts of boiling water for fifteen minutes, drain and rinse. Set aside.

3. *Salad:* As spaghetti cooks, tear six leaves romaine lettuce, first washing them thoroughly. To this in a large bowl, add a tablespoon of anchovy paste, one minced clove of garlic, a tablespoon olive oil, the juice of one lemon, two ounces parmesan cheese (grated), one raw egg, salt and freshly-ground black pepper, six croutons, and toss lightly until all lettuce is coated. Serve as is from bowl.

4. Pour sauce over spaghetti and serve immediately with salad on same plate.

5. *Espresso and Ice Cream:* Follow directions on label for making instant espresso and serve with ice cream as dessert.

Note: Purchase or defrost two centre loin pork chops for tomorrow's recipe.

6

Grapefruit Sections
Stuffed Pork Chops
   with Mushroom Gravy
Creamed Corn
Baked Apples and Honey

Approximate cooking time: 30 minutes

Ingredients:

1 grapefruit, pink or yellow
2 centre loin pork chops, 1 inch
   thick
2 apples

2 ounces honey
1 can creamed corn
1 package prepared stuffing
1 can mushroom gravy

Note: You will need two small skewers.

Preparation and cooking steps:

1. Preheat oven to 350 degrees.

2. *Pork Chops:* Cut off most of the fat from the chops. Cut a pocket in each
   chop and then stuff pockets with as much stuffing as possible and close
   openings with the small skewers. Heat three tablespoons of oil in electric or
   frying pan, add chops, and sauté for five minutes each side or until golden
   brown. Pour mushroom gravy over chops and heat another ten minutes
   at simmer setting.

3. *Grapefruit and Corn:* While the meat cooks, prepare grapefruit and corn.
   Cut grapefruit in half and cut around each section with a small knife to
   loosen the meat. Open corn and heat over low heat on stove. While corn
   heats and meat cooks, eat grapefruit.

4. *Baked Apples:* Cut the skin of the top third of each apple and pare sides
   of apple skin away from the pulp. Score the top of the apples with a knife.
   Pour an ounce of honey over each, place on small pie tin, and bake in the
   oven for ten minutes or until the apples are soft and well-cooked.

Note: Purchase or defrost three-quarters of a pound of chicken livers for
tomorrow's recipe.

7

Iced Tea
Chicken Livers with Bacon
Stir-fried Pea Pods
    with Slivered Almonds
Mandarin Oranges

Approximate preparation and cooking time: 45 minutes

Ingredients:

1 jar of iced tea mix
¾ pound of chicken livers
6 slices bacon
1 package Chinese pea pods

1 package slivered almonds
1 can of Mandarin oranges
Soy sauce
1 medium onion

Preparation and cooking steps:

1. *Livers:* Fry bacon, drain on paper towel, and set aside. Then dredge chicken livers in flour, salt and pepper to taste, and cook in frying pan in leftover bacon fat. Add soy sauce to taste. Cook for five minutes at medium heat and then add pea pods and cooked bacon, some almonds and soy sauce again, and set heat to high, stirring frequently, for another five minutes. Serve immediately.

2. *Iced Tea:* Follow directions on the jar, or, if you want to make it fresh, simply boil water, add tea, allow to steep, add three or four ice cubes, lemon juice, and sugar.

3. *Oranges:* Open can and serve in small bowls, slightly chilled.

Note: Purchase or defrost a half pound of ground beef for tomorrow's recipe.

Apple Juice
Hamburger Patties and Eggs
Hot Butterscotch Custard

Approximate preparation and cooking time: 30 minutes

Ingredients:

1 can apple juice (small)
½ pound of ground beef
3 eggs

1 package butterscotch custard
Worcestershire sauce, soy sauce,
    barbecue salt, salt and pepper

Preparation and cooking steps:

1. *Hamburger and Eggs:* Shape patties of ground beef, first adding one egg, Worcestershire and soy sauce, barbecue salt, salt and pepper to taste. Place patties in frying pan over high heat and fry until centres are cooked (about ten minutes). Place to one side and keep warm. Fry the eggs in the remaining fat, sunny side up, and serve immediately with the hamburgers.

2. *Butterscotch Custard:* Follow the instructions for preparation on the box, but halve the recipe, or quarter it, depending on whether you are cooking for one or two. Serve immediately, hot.

Note: Purchase or defrost one pound salmon for tomorrow's recipe.

Onion Soup
Salmon Steak
Broiled Tomatoes and Cheese
Strawberry Sundae

Approximate cooking and preparation time: 30 minutes

Ingredients:

1 pound fresh salmon, cut into
   1-inch thick steaks
1 lemon
Worcestershire sauce, salt, paprika,
   pepper, margarine

1 jar strawberry jam
2 tomatoes
2 slices processed cheese
Ice cream

Preparation and cooking steps:

1. Preheat oven to 400 degrees.

2. *Salmon:* Melt one-quarter cup margarine, add juice of one lemon and other spices called for above, in moderation. Coat the salmon steaks in the mixture, and place in a shallow baking pan in preheated oven for fifteen minutes on each side, or until fish flakes easily with fork.

3. *Soup:* Open and heat a can of onion soup. Eat while the salmon cooks.

4. *Tomatoes:* Cut off the tops of tomatoes and scoop out the seeds. Dice the cheese and place half the diced cheese into each tomato. Place in the oven on a pie tin and bake the same length of time the salmon cooks on one side (fifteen minutes) or until cheese bubbles.

5. *Sundae:* Take any ice cream from the freezer and spoon onto it two tablespoons of strawberry jam.

10

Hot Coffee
Rocky Mountain Eggs
Baked French Fries with Ketchup
Wild Blueberries in Cream

Approximate preparation and cooking time: 35 minutes

Ingredients:

Coffee
6 eggs
4 slices fresh white bread
2 large potatoes
1 package wild blueberries (canned
    or frozen)

1 pint cereal cream
Salt and pepper
Sugar

Preparation and cooking steps:

1. Preheat oven to 500 degrees.

2. *Potatoes:* Peel potatoes and boil for five minutes in a large pot (two quarts boiling water). Remove and cut into four-inch-long, one-inch-wide slices. Grease cookie sheet and place potato slices in oven at highest level and bake for one-half hour, turning when browned on one side, salting to taste.

3. Preheat electric frying pan or large saucepan to medium heat.

4. *Eggs:* With a small drinking glass, cut holes in the centre of each slice of bread, and discard circles from centre. Beat two eggs in a bowl, salt and pepper to taste, and, using a whisk, brush beaten egg onto the bread slices which you have placed on waxed paper, turning when one side of the bread slices is completely coated. Take care to coat only enough to cover, not to make the bread soggy. Place the bread slices in margarine in the frying pan and carefully break one egg into each of the open circles. Cover and let cook for about four to five minutes, or until the whites are firm. Then uncover, and with a spatula quickly but gently flip the slices of bread over, taking care to avoid breaking the eggs within the centre of each. Serve immediately with potatoes hot from the oven.

5. *Blueberries:* Place one cup of frozen or canned blueberries in a cup and pour cereal cream over them, adding sugar to taste. With the frozen ones, allow time for them to thaw, and for the canned ones, refreezing of leftovers is possible.

Note: Shred three slices of bread and leave out overnight for tomorrow's recipe. Allow two Cornish game hens to thaw overnight for tomorrow's recipe. Allow prepared stuffing from Menu 6, in freezer, to thaw for tomorrow's recipe.

11

Onion Soup
Stuffed Cornish Game Hen
Bacon Broccoli
Cherries Jubilee

Approximate preparation and cooking time: 60 minutes

Ingredients:

Margarine, salt, pepper, prepared
  mustard
Tarragon, sage
Prepared stuffing
2 Cornish game hens
Soy sauce
1 can condensed onion soup
1 package frozen broccoli

12 slices bacon
1 bunch green onions
Bread crumbs
1 can pitted cherries
Ice cream (vanilla)
1 can prepared whipped cream
1 bottle Kirsch (cherry brandy)
2 teaspoons cornstarch

Preparation and cooking steps:

1. Preheat oven to 350 degrees.

2. *Soup:* Open can and prepare soup according to directions on can. Serve just before birds are done.

3. *Birds:* Carefully wash each bird and remove bag of internal organs from chest cavity. Season cavity of each bird and put a pat of margarine into the chest cavities. Stuff cavities with prepared stuffing and skewer the openings shut. Place in the oven on a roasting pan, or in a pie plate, greased, for fifty minutes. Prepare a baste for the birds of one-quarter cup melted margarine, plus pinches of salt, freshly ground pepper, mustard, tarragon, and sage. Baste the birds frequently.

4. *Broccoli:* While the birds cook, cook broccoli in two quarts of boiling salted water until tender and drain off the water. At same time, cook bacon slices in saucepan, then add one cup minced green onions and a cup of dry bread crumbs and stir-fry in hot bacon fat until lightly browned. Keep hot and serve with birds when done.

5. *Cherries Jubilee:* Drain syrup from the can of pitted cherries into a saucepan, heat to a boil and add cornstarch and one tablespoon water (mixed beforehand). Cook until thickened, add cherries and cook another ten minutes. Warm one-third cup of cherry brandy in a saucepan and put two large scoops of ice cream into separate bowls. Pour hot cherry sauce over ice cream and then warmed brandy, which you have ignited just before pouring over. This should be done at the table, following the main course.

Note: Save remaining green onions; buy and defrost two pounds chicken wings for tomorrow's recipe.

12

Sweet and Sour Chicken Wings
Chinese Rice
Watermelon Balls

Approximate preparation and cooking time: 30 minutes

Ingredients:

2 pounds chicken wings
1 cup rice
½ watermelon
2 eggs

3 green onions*
1 can prepared sweet and sour sauce
Soy sauce, salt and pepper
4 ounces honey

Preparation and cooking steps:

1. Preheat oven to 250 degrees.

2. *Rice:* Boil one cup of rice in two cups of salted water for twenty minutes. Drain excess water. Beat eggs and fry in oil in saucepan or electric frying pan until firm, shredding as the eggs fry. To this, add sliced green onions, stirring constantly over high heat until cooked. Add rice and mix in soy sauce and salt and pepper to taste, again stirring constantly until rice is hot. Place in an ovenproof bowl in the oven to keep warm until chicken wings are done.

3. *Chicken:* In the same frying pan, fry the chicken wings until well-browned on all sides (about ten minutes). Then open a can of sweet and sour sauce and add to the wings, stirring constantly. Next add honey and two ounces of soy sauce and cook for ten minutes or until mixture becomes thick and sticky. Serve immediately with rice hot from the oven.

4. *Watermelon:* While the chicken cooks, scoop watermelon into balls after first removing seeds. Place the balls in the freezer to firm up before serving.

Note: Buy and defrost four chicken breasts needed for tomorrow's recipe.
*Save leftover green onions for tomorrow's recipe.

Vegetable Soup
Chicken Burgers
Potato Salad
Apples and Cheese

Approximate preparation and cooking time: 45 minutes

Ingredients:

1 can vegetable soup	2 ounces cheddar cheese
4 chicken breasts	4 eggs
2 large potatoes	Bread crumbs
Mayonnaise	Salt and pepper
Green onions	2 stalks of celery, diced
2 apples	Ketchup and mustard

Preparation and cooking steps:

1. *Soup:* Open can of soup, heat and serve.

2. *Chicken:* Bone chicken breasts (see instructions on page 127), remove the skin, and finely mince the chicken into a paste. Then add bread crumbs (your own or prepared), two eggs, salt and pepper to the mixture and form into balls. Heat electric skillet or frying pan to high heat and fry the chicken balls (squashed) in hot oil, turning when brown on one side. Takes about fifteen minutes. Place patties on hamburger buns, add ketchup and mustard to taste.

3. *Potato Salad:* While preparing chicken, boil two quarts salted water, peel the potatoes, and boil them in the water until tender. Then dice the potatoes into one-inch cubes. In the same water, hardboil two eggs. This takes about ten minutes. Shell the eggs and mince. To the diced potatoes and minced eggs in a large bowl, add diced onions, salt, pepper, celery, and mayonnaise; refrigerate until the meat is cooked. Serve immediately with the meat on the same plate, with apples and cheese on the side as a dessert.

Note: Buy and defrost a package of cod fillets for tomorrow's recipe.

52

14

Tomato Juice
Fish Chowder
Green Peas
Pears and Cheese

Approximate preparation and cooking time: 20 minutes

Ingredients:

2 cans of tomato juice (small)
2 cans of prepared Boston clam
    chowder
1 package of cod fillets
1 can of green peas

2 pears
2 ounces of cheddar cheese
Salt and pepper
Hot rolls (buy fresh)

Preparation and cooking steps:

1. Preheat oven to 250 degrees and warm bread rolls.

2. *Fish:* Brown fish fillets in oil in frying pan, five minutes each side, salt and pepper to taste, and cut into one-inch sections (either before or after cooking). Open cans of chowder and add to the mixture, cooking another five minutes. Serve immediately, with hot bread rolls on side and pears and cheese as dessert.

Note: Purchase or defrost two pounds of chicken drumsticks for tomorrow's recipe.

 Cream of Mushroom Soup
Broiled Chicken Drumsticks
Baked French Fries
Pound Cake and Custard Sauce

Approximate preparation and cooking time: 45 minutes

Ingredients:

1 can condensed cream of
   mushroom soup
2 pounds of chicken drumsticks
   (approx. 8)

2 large potatoes
1 small pound cake (prepared)
1 package custard

Preparation and cooking steps:

1. Preheat the oven to 500 degrees.

2. *Soup:* Open can, heat soup following directions, and serve just before eating chicken.

3. *Chicken:* Salt and pepper chicken, place in oven on baking sheet on highest grid. Broil for approximately fifteen to twenty minutes, turning frequently until brown. Remove and serve immediately with French fries.

4. *Potatoes:* Boil salted water (two quarts), peel potatoes, and boil potatoes for five minutes. Remove from water, cut into four-inch-long by one-inch-wide slices, grease cookie sheet, and place potatoes on sheet along side the chicken, turning frequently until brown, about twenty minutes. Remove and serve hot with chicken.

5. *Pound Cake and Custard Sauce:* Cut slices of pound cake as required. Heat pudding mix following directions, using half of ingredients listed. When hot, pour over pound cake and serve.

Note: Shop for or defrost one pound beef stewing meat for tomorrow's recipe.

16

Cream of Celery Soup
Beef Stew
Cheese Cauliflower
Spiced Peaches

Approximate preparation and cooking time: 40 minutes

Ingredients:

1 can cream of celery soup	Soy sauce
1 pound beef stewing meat	Flour
1 clove garlic	1 small cauliflower
1 medium onion	2 slices processed cheese
3 carrots	1 can peaches
2 stalks of celery	Cinnamon and cloves, powdered
2 potatoes	*Note:* You will need a pressure
Salt, pepper	cooker.

Preparation and cooking steps:

1. Set oven to broil.

2. *Soup:* Open can, heat and serve as directed on the label, while stew cooks.

3. *Stew:* First coat cubed stewing meat in flour and salt and pepper to taste. Then heat oil and brown cubes of beef in oil for three to five minutes in pressure cooker. Dice carrots, celery, and potatoes and mince garlic clove. Add vegetables to meat in cooker, add two-thirds cup of water and cook over high heat on the stove until pressure gauge begins to whistle. Then set the heat to medium and cook another ten to twelve minutes in the pressure cooker. Remove the pressure cooker from the heat and plunge it immediately under cold running tap water until the pressure is removed (press down on pressure gauge with a knife to remove completely the inner pressure). Remove cover and set aside.

4. *Cauliflower:* While the meat is cooking, place a small cauliflower in two quarts of boiling, salted water and cook for ten to fifteen minutes or until the cauliflower is tender. Drain. Set the cauliflower in a pie tin or casserole dish and brush with margarine. Put processed cheese on top and broil in the oven until done (about five minutes). This should be served still hot with the stew.

5. *Peaches:* Open a small can of peaches, spice as desired with cinnamon and cloves.

Note: Buy or defrost a three-pound chuck roast for tomorrow's recipe.

17

Beef with Barley Soup
Chuck Roast, Pressure Cooked
Rice in Gravy
Apple Pie
Coffee

Approximate preparation and cooking time: 45 minutes

Ingredients:

1 can beef and barley soup	3 carrots
1 three-pound chuck roast	3 stalks of celery
1 cup of rice	1 apple pie, prepared
1 medium onion	2 potatoes

Preparation and cooking steps:

1. Preheat the oven to 350 degrees.

2. Make coffee.

3. *Vegetables:* Peel potatoes, dice carrots in one-inch pieces, dice onion, dice celery.

4. *Soup:* Open can and heat soup; serve while roast and rice cook.

5. *Roast:* Brown the roast quickly in oil over high heat in pressure cooker on top of stove, lid off. Add one cup of water and seal, heating on high heat until the pressure gauge whistles, then turning to medium heat. Cook a total of thirty minutes. Cool, remove from cooker in the same way as with Beef Stew in Menu 16. Keep warm in a casserole dish in the oven. And if possible, save about two ounces of gravy for tomorrow's recipe.

6. *Vegetables:* Return diced vegetables to the pressure cooker in the remaining gravy and reseal cooker. Cook five minutes from when the pressure gauge whistles and heat is reduced. Remove and cool in same way as Menu 16, then take off lid. When the vegetables are done, add them to the casserole in the oven, leaving half the gravy in the cooker.

7. *Boiled Rice:* While roast cooks, boil rice in two quarts of boiling, salted water until done (about twenty minutes) and add the rice to the gravy in the cooker after the vegetables have been removed and reheat. Serve immediately with the roast and vegetables in the casserole. Cut the meat directly at the table on a cutting board or serving plate as needed.

8. Serve prepared apple pie and coffee for dessert.

Note: Buy but do not defrost one package frozen strawberries for tomorrow's recipe.

18

Beer or Ale
Hot Roast Beef Sandwich
Honeyed Carrots
Strawberry Shortcake

Approximate preparation and cooking time: 30 minutes

Ingredients:

Beer or ale
Bread
Carrots
Honey
Salt and pepper
1 package frozen strawberries

1 can instant whipped cream
1 jar strawberry jam (should have
    leftover from Menu 9)
6 chiffon cupcakes (prepared)
1 can prepared beef gravy
2 ounces honey

Preparation and cooking steps:

1. *Shortcake:* Prepare this part first. Cut cupcakes in half and spread a thick layer of strawberry jam on each half. Cut half of the frozen strawberries into thin slices and store remainder in the refrigerator for use in Menu 21. Place the strawberry slices on the bottom layers of the cupcakes. Spread a thick layer of whipped cream on the sliced strawberries and replace the top half of the cupcakes. Put a thick dab of whipped cream on top of each cupcake and add a whole strawberry, uncut, to each. Chill in refrigerator until needed.

2. *Sandwich:* Slice remaining roast from Menu 17 and place on slices of bread. Open the can of prepared gravy and add leftover gravy from Menu 17. Heat and keep hot.

3. *Carrots:* Boil three carrots sliced into three-inch chunks in salted water for ten minutes or until tender. Drain and add honey and heat until all carrot pieces are coated and glazed.

4. Pour gravy over the sliced meat on bread. Place a bread slice on the sandwich and pour gravy over it also. Serve immediately with the hot glazed carrots.

Note: Buy and defrost one package frozen halibut fillets for use in tomorrow's recipe.

19

New England Clam Chowder
Cheese and Tomato Fish
Stewed Tomatoes
Rice Pudding

Approximate preparation and cooking time: 60 to 90 minutes

Ingredients:

1 can New England clam chowder	Sugar
1 package halibut fillets	Flour
4 slices processed cheese	1 quart whole milk
4 medium tomatoes	Margarine
1 can tomato soup	½ cup raisins
1 cup of rice	Nutmeg and cinnamon
Vanilla	

Preparation and cooking steps:

1. Preheat oven to 350 degrees.

2. *Rice:* Boil rice as in previous recipes.

3. *Soup:* Following directions on can of clam chowder, heat and serve soup once fish is in the oven.

4. *Fish:* Coat fish in flour, salt and pepper to taste. Brown the fish in oil in frying pan. Place the fish in a baking dish and pour a can of tomato soup over it and set it aside for a moment.

5. *Tomatoes:* Cut tomatoes in halves, removing seeds. Place these sections over the fish and bake in oven for twenty minutes or until fish flakes easily and tomatoes are tender. Remove the fish from the oven and put processed cheese over the fish and return to the oven, baking for ten more minutes or until the cheese melts and begins to bubble. Serve immediately.

6. *Rice Pudding:* While the fish bakes, mix the boiled rice with two tablespoons of moistened sugar, and a quart of milk. Stir in one ounce of margarine, the raisins, a pinch of nutmeg and cinnamon, and a dash of vanilla. Place the rice mixture in a pie dish. Bake for one hour in the oven or until golden brown and serve hot. The leftovers are a great snack.

Note: Buy or defrost two rib or loin lamb chops for tomorrow's recipe.

20

Hawaiian Punch
Lamb Chops
Rice Pilaf
Pear Halves

Approximate preparation and cooking time: 30 minutes

Ingredients:

2 rib or loin lamb chops
Salt and pepper
1 can pear halves
1 jar currant jelly

1 package prepared rice pilaf
1 tin Hawaiian Punch
Shortening

Preparation and cooking steps:

1. Preheat the oven to broil temperature for ten minutes.

2. *Rice:* Follow directions on package. Cooks in about twenty minutes in boiling water.

3. *Lamb:* Snip fat on chops at one-inch intervals to prevent curling in broiling. Season meat to taste. Rub broiling pan with fat or shortening to prevent sticking and set lamb on pan at the highest rack setting. Broil for ten minutes, approximately, on each side. When done, serve with rice pilaf.

4. *Pears:* Open can of pears, drain half pears and juice and store the rest in refrigerator for use in Menu 25. Fill centre of each pear half with currant jelly and serve as dessert.

Note: Buy or defrost a package of boned fast-fry pork chops for tomorrow's recipe.

21

Fruit Cup
Fast-Fry Pork Chops,
    Mushroom Gravy
Sauerkraut
Tarts
Coffee

Approximate preparation and cooking time: 35 minutes

Ingredients:

1 can fruit cocktail
1 package boned fast-fry pork
    chops (6)
1 can mushroom gravy
1 jar or can prepared sauerkraut

6 prepared tart shells
Strawberries and strawberry jam,
    from Menu 18
Salt and pepper

Preparation and cooking steps:

1. Preheat oven to 350 degrees and bake tart shells as per directions on box. When done, remove from the oven and cool.

2. Make coffee.

3. *Fruit Cup:* Open can of fruit cocktail and serve as an appetizer in small bowls. Reserve remainder for use in Menu 25.

4. *Pork:* Fry seasoned pork chops in oil in electric frying pan or large frying pan on the stove for approximately ten minutes each side, or until golden brown. Open the can of gravy and pour it over the chops in the pan and cook for another five minutes, stirring frequently to avoid burning. Serve chops immediately with sauerkraut right from the jar. Store the remainder of the sauerkraut for future use in Menu 29.

5. *Tarts:* Spoon strawberries into baked tart shells. Spoon strawberry jam over the strawberries. Place in the oven and reheat for about five minutes, or until the jam begins to bubble. Serve while hot, with coffee as dessert.

Note: Remove wild blueberries left over from Menu 10 from the freezer and defrost for tomorrow's recipe. Buy or defrost one pound of ground beef.

22

Beef Vegetable Soup
Meat Loaf
Mixed Vegetables
Wild Blueberries and Ice Cream

Approximate preparation and cooking time: 30 minutes

Ingredients:

1 pound ground beef
Salt and pepper
1 clove garlic
1 medium onion
1 beaten egg
Bread crumbs or crushed Cornflakes

¼ teaspoon dry mustard
4 ounces prepared ketchup
1 can mixed vegetables
Wild blueberries
Ice cream

Preparation and cooking steps:

1. Preheat oven to 425 degrees.

2. *Meat Loaf:* Chop onion and garlic finely and add the beef, egg, mustard, bread crumbs, ketchup, salt, and pepper. Bake in the oven wrapped in aluminum foil shaped into loaf form or in a loaf pan or baking dish for about thirty minutes. Unwrap, keep warm, and, when the vegetables are ready, slice and serve.

3. *Vegetables:* Open a can of mixed vegetables and heat. Serve while hot with meat loaf fresh from the oven.

4. *Wild Blueberries and Ice Cream:* Scoop ice cream on hand from freezer into bowls and spoon blueberries onto the ice cream. Serve immediately after main course.

Note: Buy and defrost two chicken breasts for tomorrow's recipe. As only two breasts are needed, refreeze the remaining breasts in the package for future use, or cook with the others and use as a snack.

23

Beef Consomme with Green Onions
Chinese Stir-Fry Dinner
Chinese Rice
Dried Figs
Tea

Approximate preparation and cooking time: 30 minutes

Ingredients:

1 can of beef consomme
Tea
Green onions
1 cup rice
Soy sauce
1 package dried figs
1 package frozen Chinese pea pods
8 ounces fresh or canned bean
    sprouts

1 green pepper
1 medium onion
4 ounces medium fresh or canned
    mushrooms
2 chicken breasts, boned
Salt and pepper
Peanut oil

Preparation and cooking steps:

1. *Soup:* Empty can into saucepan and heat. While it heats, slice very thinly two green onions and toss into the soup. Season with soy sauce and serve hot, after vegetables for stir-fry have been prepared but before frying pan has preheated.

2. *Chinese Dinner:*
   a) Chinese Rice: see Menu 12 for preparation.
   b) Heat electric frying pan to highest setting. Add peanut oil and allow to heat. While heating, slice onion and dice it, chop finely three more green onions, open can of bean sprouts, thinly slice the mushrooms, and cut green pepper into chunks, first removing all seeds and pith. Fry in oil until onions glaze. Add boned chicken cut into strips and Chinese pea pods. Stir frequently over high heat until all vegetables are coated with hot oil and are cooked to taste but still crisp. Serve immediately with Chinese rice.

3. *Tea and Figs:* Make tea in usual fashion and serve with dried figs as dessert. Store leftover figs in the refrigerator for use as a snack.

Note: Save remaining tea for use in Menu 24.

24

Iced Tea
Tuna-Noodle Casserole
Green Peas
Grapes

Approximate preparation time: 1 hour

Ingredients:

Tea
1 large can of drained, flaked tuna
1 can of green peas
1 can of condensed cream of
   mushroom soup
1 small onion
¼ cup margarine

1 cup grated cheddar cheese
1 can sliced pimentos
1 small package of potato chips
2 green onions
1 lemon
1 package elbow noodles
Grapes, red and green

Preparation and cooking steps:

1. Preheat oven to 375 degrees.

2. *Iced Tea:* Make strong tea in the usual way (or use leftover tea in fridge), then add juice of one lemon and sugar to taste. Serve with ice in a tall glass.

3. *Tuna:* Combine in a bowl the tuna, soup, onion (minced), margarine, cheese, two pimentos from the can (minced), potato chips (crush them), and two finely sliced green onions. Boil the noodles in two quarts of boiling, salted water for about twenty minutes, or until soft. Drain and rinse. Combine the noodles and a can of green peas with the other ingredients in an oven-proof casserole, greased, and bake for thirty-five minutes in the oven, or until golden brown on top and bubbling. Serve immediately.

4. *Grapes:* Serve grapes on a separate plate as dessert.

Note: Put the leftover grapes aside in the refrigerator for use in Menu 25. Put the rest of the pimentos aside also, for use in Menu 27. Store the pimentos in a bowl, not in the can they came in, or they will get a tinny taste.

25

Pineapple Juice
Fruit Salad Plate
Lemon-Honey Dressing

Approximate preparation time: 20 minutes

Ingredients:

1 small can of pineapple juice
Fruit cocktail (left from Menu 21)
Pear halves (left from Menu 20)

Grapes (left from Menu 24)
4 ounces of honey
1 lemon

Preparation steps:

1. *Juice:* Open juice can and serve chilled in a small glass or glasses as required. Store remaining juice for snack.

2. *Fruit Salad:* Combine fruit in a large bowl, and toss thoroughly with the juice of one lemon and honey. Place in freezer for five minutes to chill and serve immediately.

Note: Purchase or defrost one pound of ground beef for tomorrow's recipe.

26

Tacos
Spanish Rice
Refried Beans
Fresh Fruit

Approximate preparation and cooking time: 45 minutes

Ingredients:

1 package of prepared taco shells
   (6 - 8)
1 brick of mild cheddar cheese
1 head of lettuce
1 can of taco sauce
Oil
2 medium tomatoes
1 pound ground beef

Mayonnaise
Salt and pepper
1 medium onion
1 cup of rice
1 can of refried beans
Fruit (assorted)
1 package prepared chili mix

Preparation and cookings steps:

1. *Beans:* Open and heat can of refried beans, adding a little cooking oil to make them more pliable. Salt to taste. Add a little grated cheese if desired.

2. *Rice:* See Menu 4 and add remainder of pimento from Menu 24.

3. *Tacos:* Chop onion and fry with the beef in oil in a large frying pan or electric frying pan, adding sauce and powdered chili mix, then simmering slowly for ten minutes. Keep warm. Shred lettuce and cheese and cut tomatoes into chunks while beef simmers. Spoon hot beef mixture into the prepared taco shells, add the tomato chunks, shredded lettuce and mayonnaise, and serve hot with rice and refried beans. Fruit is a refreshing dessert with this "hot" dish.

Note: Purchase or defrost two pounds of cross-cut beef shanks for tomorrow's recipe.

27

Ale or Beer
Simmered Beef Shanks
Green Beans Pimento
Mandarin Oranges

Approximate preparation and cooking time: 90 minutes

Ingredients:

2 pounds cross-cut beef shanks
Flour
Oil
Tomato juice

2 large potatoes
1 can of Mandarin oranges
1 can of green beans with pimento
Basil

Preparation and cooking steps:

1. *Meat:* Dust with flour, and salt and pepper the meat to taste. Brown the meat in hot oil in your pressure cooker. Add a half cup of water, seal the cooker and heat over high heat until the gauge whistles. Reduce the heat to medium and cook twenty minutes. Cool under tap water, remove lid and set meat aside, keeping it warm on the stove, in a small saucepan. In the remaining liquid gravy left in the pressure cooker, place potatoes sliced in chunks, and one-third cup tomato juice. Reseal the pressure cooker, heat and follow gauge, reaching pressure and reduce heat. Cool under tap water, open cooker, add meat again, and bring to a boil on top of stove with cover off.

2. *Beans:* Open and heat the can of beans. Serve while hot with the shanks.

3. *Dessert:* Open and serve can of Mandarin oranges as desired. Perhaps a squirt of canned whipped cream, stored in the refrigerator from previous menus, would add a nice touch.

Note: Purchase, fresh from the butcher, four ounces of turkey roll.

28

Turkey Noodle Soup
Cold Meat Plate
Potato Salad
Tomato Juice
Sliced Bananas

Approximate preparation and cooking time: 30 minutes

Ingredients:

1 can of turkey noodle soup
1 package of processed ham
   (4 ounces)
1 package of processed salami
   (4 ounces)
4 ounces turkey roll, fresh from
   butcher

2 tomatoes
4 ounces of sharp cheddar cheese
2 potatoes
Mayonnaise
Green onions

Preparation and cooking steps:

1. *Soup:* Heat can of soup in a saucepan and serve just after arranging meats and vegetables on the plate.

2. *Potato Salad:* See Menu 13. Once prepared (about twenty minutes), arrange the potato salad in centre of serving plate.

3. *Meat Plate:* Slice meat and cheese in long, four-inch by one-half-inch strips. (All meat, it should be noted, can either be bought in four-ounce portions fresh from the supermarket's meat counter, or in packages, with the exception of the turkey roll, which can only be bought fresh. If no fresh turkey roll is available, use another prepared meat, such as head cheese, which is available in a four-ounce package as well.) Slice the tomato into chunks, and arrange with the meat around the potato salad. Serve. Save the leftovers as a base for Menu 29.

4. *Bananas:* Slice and serve bananas as dessert. Cream may be added with sugar if you wish.

Chicken Noodle Soup
Clubhouse Sandwich
Sauerkraut
Cookies

Approximate preparation and cooking time: 20 minutes

Ingredients:

1 can chicken noodle soup
1 loaf sliced white bread
Bacon
Turkey, ham, and meats leftover
    from Menu 28
Mayonnaise
1 head lettuce, small

1 tomato
Margarine
Sliced pickles (sweet or dill),
    optional
1 small bag potato chips, flavour
    optional

Preparation and cooking steps:

1. Cook the bacon in saucepan until crisp and drain fat.

2. *Soup:* Open can of soup, heat and serve.

3. *Sandwich:* Cut crusts off six slices of bread. Toast the slices in an electric toaster or in the oven until golden brown. Coat each slice on one side with margarine. Top first slice of toast for each of the two sandwiches with lettuce and turkey. Then spread mayonnaise on top. Top each with a second toast slice. Add sliced tomato, bacon pieces, sliced pickles, and ham and salami slices. Top with the third slice of toast for each sandwich, anchor each with a toothpick, cut in half cross-wise or diagonally, and serve with chips.

4. *Sauerkraut:* Serve sandwich with side helping of sauerkraut, leftover from Menu 21.

5. *Cookies* are a light dessert.

30

Orange Juice
Cheese Muffins
Sour Cream
Baked Candy Apples

Approximate preparation and cooking time: 35 minutes

Ingredients:

1 pint sour cream
12 ounces dry cottage cheese
Sugar
Margarine
2 eggs
1 cup flour (all-purpose)

2 teaspoons baking powder
1 small can orange juice (sweetened
     or unsweetened)
6 caramel toffees
2 large red apples

Preparation and cooking steps:

1. Preheat oven to 400 degrees and grease a muffin tin and a small pie plate.

2. *Muffins:* In a large mixing bowl, combine cottage cheese, three tablespoons of sugar, one-half cup of margarine, eggs, flour, baking powder, and a pinch of salt, and mix together thoroughly. Pour mixture into greased muffin tin and bake for twenty minutes. Serve the cheese buns hot from the oven, spooning cold sour cream over them.

3. *Apples:* While muffins are baking, core apples and peel the top third. Score the tops of each apple with a knife before placing in the oven. Bake for twenty minutes, or until apples are soft. While apples bake, slowly heat caramel toffee squares (one inch each square) in a saucepan with a tiny splash of milk. Once melted, simmer until bubbling, and then set on warm setting. Remove apples and cheese buns from the oven. Pour hot caramel sauce over the baked apples and serve immediately.

Notes

Cooking for Crowds

There is an art to cooking for crowds. This chapter will devote considerable time to the mechanics of cooking and planning meals for many people.

The goal in cooking for crowds is to please your guests with an inventive menu while still being able to enjoy your own party. This takes careful planning, and you will be learning all about serving, quantities, kinds of parties, and other details as you read along.

Whom you invite is up to you, but far more important is your ability to be a good host. To do this you must pay attention to small details, details which often make the difference between a successful and unsuccessful affair.

The number to invite is the first decision. The answer depends on available space, how many you can handle smoothly and your purpose for giving the party. Until you become familiar with party-giving, try a rough estimate, based on what you think that you can handle in the space available and start planning from there. This will determine the kind of party you have. For six or eight, you can easily have a dinner party; a few more and you have the makings of a buffet supper; for larger numbers, an open house or cocktail party might serve your plans better.

Depending on your schedule and the schedules of your friends, a party can be held any time of the day. You may want to plan a lunch, brunch, open house, potluck party, informal supper, dinner party, barbecue, cocktail party, or a late-night supper party.

The time of day will also dictate what you will serve. A noon-time party usually means a luncheon, while a mid-morning party can be brunch. Eight in the evening customarily means a dinner party, while a cocktail party is held in the evening or late afternoon, depending on what you are planning to do or where you are planning to go for the rest of the evening.

Lunch usually means light food, brunch even lighter fare, while dinner means considerably more preparation for you. Note here that the people you have decided to invite also influence the food you plan to serve; so keep in mind personal preferences as well as any dietary limitations of your guests.

There are two cooking philosophies, formal and informal, to guide you when planning a party. If formal, you prepare the food beforehand, whereas you involve your guests in the food preparation of an informal party.

Which to choose depends on your own personal preference, but both are fun to try. If you are trying the former, remember to choose only one new dish for each affair. That way if your new dish does not turn out, the whole meal is not spoiled! Other dishes should be ones you have made successfully. For the bachelor relatively new to cooking, the more informal affair lends itself nicely to having his friends over. The informality lets the bachelor share in the cooking responsibilities and thus have more time to relax and enjoy his guests.

The Mongolian or Chinese Hot Pot is ideal for your first informal affair. It is a meal in itself and perfect to serve to six to eight people after a show or before relaxing for an evening in front of a television set or stereo. All that is involved here is slicing the meat and making the sauces. Guests can cook and eat all evening long, not at any particular sitting. Using several fondue pots, or if you can manage to find one, a real Mongolian hot pot, simmer chicken broth made by you (see next chapter) or brought by someone else, or canned, and let your guests drop a few food tidbits at a time into the hot broth with chopsticks or fondue forks. They can fish them out whenever they think the tidbits are done to their individual liking and dip them into a variety of sauces you have made. Fluffy rice, kept hot in a chafing dish or in a casserole in the oven, is an ideal accompaniment. Mongolian Hot Pot is a deliciously informal idea, right down to the cooking broth which is often served as the highlight of the meal, after all the tidbits are cooked, as it captures all the cooking flavours of the many ingredients.

The following is a list of what you will need for this kind of party to serve six guests:

Mongolian Hot Pot

Ingredients:

¾ pound large raw shrimp, shelled
2 uncooked chicken breasts, boned
½ head Chinese cabbage
1½ cups halved mushrooms, fresh or canned
4 cups small spinach leaves, stems removed
1 five-ounce can water chestnuts, drained and thinly sliced
1 bag or can bean sprouts, drained
40 ounces chicken broth, fresh or canned
1 tablespoon grated ginger root, or 1½ teaspoon ginger powder
Soy sauce, prepared horseradish, chili sauce, sugar, Tabasco sauce, lemon
    juice, garlic, dry mustard, salt, salad oil, peanut butter, ketchup

Preparation and cooking steps:

1. Slice the chicken into long, thin strips.
2. Cut the vegetables as directed above.

3. Arrange the meat, vegetables, and shrimp on a large platter.

4. Heat the chicken broth in fondue pots or hot pot and keep at simmer.

5. Make the sauces:
   a) Chinese Mustard Sauce: boil ½ cup water and add to it ¼ cup dry mustard, ½ tsp. salt, 1 tbsp. salad oil.
   b) Ginger Sauce: boil ½ cup soy sauce and 1½ tsp. ground ginger or 1 tbsp. grated ginger root.
   c) Peanut Sauce: blend until smooth, ¼ cup peanut butter, 2 tbsp. soy sauce, 1½ tsp. water, ¼ tsp. sugar, 1 drop Tabasco sauce, ½ clove minced garlic, ¼ cup water.
   d) Red Sauce: combine 3 tbsp. ketchup, 3 tbsp. chili sauce, 1½ tbsp. prepared horseradish, 1 tsp. lemon juice and several dashes Tabasco sauce.

6. Arrange the sauces in individual bowls around the meat and vegetables and shrimp.

7. Heat the chicken broth in the fondues or hot pot, and eat as desired. You will love it and so will your guests. Preparation time, by the way, is approximately one hour. Eating and cooking time is all evening!

A fondue party is similar to the hot pot party, except somewhat less of a complete meal. Perfect for after-theatre or movie gatherings, this again is ideal for six to eight people.

Fondue

Ingredients:

> 2 pounds beef tenderloin
> Cooking oil (peanut oil)
> Sour cream
> Blue cheese
> Worcestershire sauce
> Mushrooms (fresh or canned)
> Butter, lemon juice, tarragon, pepper
> Red wine
> *Note:* You will need two fondue pots.

Preparation and cooking steps:

1. Heat the oil in the fondue pots.

2. Cut the meat into one-inch cubes.

3. Make the sauces
   a) Blue Cheese Sauce: mix 1 cup sour cream with ¼ cup crumbled blue cheese and a dash of Worcestershire sauce.

b) Bordelaise Sauce: sauté ½ cup fresh or canned mushrooms in butter, mix with 3 tbsp. red wine, 2 tbsp. lemon juice, 2 tbsp. crushed tarragon (or ½ tbsp. powdered), and simmer five minutes in small saucepan.

4. Cook the meat in hot oil in fondue and dip as desired in the sauces. A tip here is to mix oil and chicken stock in equal portions. This is far less fatty, and therefore will avoid the heavy stomach feeling so common after fondues based on pure cooking oil to fry the meat.

Four other informal parties are the buffet, wine and cheese, potluck supper, and barbecue. All four are equally informal to the fondue and hot pot and just as easy to plan.

The potluck party can be anything you want it to be; the object is to eat whatever food you find yourself with after all the guests arrive! A fill-in-the-blanks potluck party is ideal: you make up the menu according to dishes, and then make a chart separating each dish on the menu. Next call up the guests to invite them, and at the same time tell them that each guest is responsible for one particular dish and ask them which dish they would like to prepare. Gradually you will have everyone bringing something on the menu. And remember to keep track of who is bringing what, because someone who has said they would make one dish might forget which it is and seek your help. Things to include in this kind of menu are a fish dish, a salad dish, a rice dish, a meat dish, a fancy dessert dish, an exotic drink, some appetizers, some fresh fruits, and some wine and/or spirits. Think up something unusual for each dish, but take care to plan dishes than can blend with one another and take it from there.

And if you want the potluck to be even more informal with a minimum of preparation for your guests, why not try the same thing with a delicatessen-style potluck. Here dishes will be easier to get or prepare, such as potato salad, smoked salmon, corned beef, roast chicken, a large salad, pickles, Greek olives, antipasto, pickled tomatoes, etc. Use your imagination or let your guests use theirs.

Buffets are equally simple to prepare and just as informal. All you will need in the way of equipment to manage successfully is a large folding table and several warming trays (or electric frying pans) to keep the dishes hot. Choose foods that are relatively easy to prepare. This can include a roast turkey (follow the directions on the plastic wrapper). Another perfect dish for buffet is:

Oriental Short Ribs

Ingredients:

    4 pounds veal short ribs
    1 can pineapple chunks
    1 can button mushrooms, drained

1 cup (8 oz.) chopped celery
1 green pepper, cut into wedges
1 red pimento, cut into slices
1 medium onion, thinly sliced
½ tsp. lemon juice
½ tsp. salt
Soy sauce
Pepper
½ tsp. ginger
2 tbsp. cornstarch
Fresh fruit, assorted

Preparation and cooking steps:

1. Preheat oven to 325 degrees.

2. Cut the vegetables as directed above.

3. Brown the ribs in hot oil in frying pan, mix with the remaining ingredients, except for the fruit.

4. Bake in casserole for one hour or until ribs are tender.

5. Serve hot at the table with the fresh fruit as a side dish. Serves six to eight people.

Wine and cheese parties are also simple to prepare. There are two ways to do them. Either buy the cheeses yourself and cut them yourself, or better yet, let a cheese specialty house recommend a selection of cheeses to please any of your guests' tastes. A specialty house does a better job because they can give you an accurate amount of cheese in sufficient variety which may save you money. Besides, they usually add some fresh fruit and the cheese board itself, which again saves you money. A word of caution: do not purchase highly aromatic cheeses because they are usually not touched by your guests and will spoil. A recommended selection of cheeses for ten people follows:

Brie	Provolone
Camembert	Swiss
Limburger	Roquefort
Edam	Stilton
Gouda	Gruyère

Wines that go with the cheeses are a matter of personal taste and a matter of a good deal of experimentation. If you can, the best way to handle this is to let your guests bring their own wines. You will need at least five different wines to serve ten people, so plan for this or ask your guests accordingly. A selection of wines could be as follows:
Reds: claret, Pinot Noir, Chianti, Zinfandel
White: Riesling, Moselle, Pouilly-Fuissé, Chablis, sauterne
Sparkling Wines: sparkling burgundy, sparkling rosé, champagne

Two other delicious informal meals can be made at the table. The first is a seafood classic, Cioppino.

Cioppino

Ingredients:

> 2 onions, diced
> 2 garlic cloves, minced
> 1 tablespoon parsley
> 2 tablespoon cooking oil
> 4 8-oz. cans tomato sauce
> 1 pound lobster, frozen or fresh
> 2 pounds crab, frozen or fresh
> ½ pound shrimp, frozen or fresh
> 1 pound white-meat fish (cod, sea bass, halibut)
> Prawns (6) if available, defrosted or fresh
> Fresh muffins, sourdough bread or cornbread

Preparation and cooking steps:

1. Cut the vegetables as directed above.

2. Sauté the onions, garlic, and parsley in oil in a dutch oven until onions are tender. Add the tomato sauce and simmer, stirring occasionally, for one and a half hours.

3. Cut the lobster in half lengthwise. Remove the crab shell and crack the claws and legs, remove the spongy parts under the shell and wash the body cavity. Clean and shell the shrimps and prawns. Cut the white fish into small chunks.

4. Add the seafood to the simmering sauce and simmer a further thirty minutes.

5. Serve hot with muffins or breads. Serves six to eight people and takes about two and a half hours to prepare leisurely.

Note: Remember to allow for overnight defrosting of your frozen ingredients, if any.

The second informal meal is Bouillabaise, a French seafood specialty renowned for its taste and uniqueness. Much more difficult and time-consuming to prepare than Cioppino, it will be included in the next chapter as a gourmet meal (Gourmet Menu 12).

The dinner party is the most involved and most exacting of any meal you might plan; the recipes for dinner parties are dealt with in detail in the next chapter, Cooking Gourmet. In fact all the recipes in the next chapter are designed especially with the dinner party for six people in mind; so when you are ready to plan one, look over the chapter carefully and choose whatever you think will suit your evening and your guests.

But now our attention in this chapter turns to other valuable tips for entertaining crowds, from table setting, serving details, and portions, to mood and decor, so that you can ably entertain crowds of up to twenty people.

Behind every successful gathering in your home or apartment is careful attention to detail, particularly in table arrangements. Of course this in turn depends on the size of your dining and entertaining facilities, but you can govern yourself by a few important pointers.

For informal gatherings, such as barbecues and fondues, you can work well within extremely limited space, seating people informally around your living room on whatever furniture you have available, and perhaps even on the floor on pillows. Overflow can be taken up on the balcony of your apartment or the patio of your house. However even with informal gatherings, it is a wise move to purchase three or four stacking chairs which you can store and take out whenever needed.

For more formal gatherings, such as brunches, lunches, and dinners, where a larger number of people are expected, you will instead have to rely on more careful planning. Assuming you have a large dining room table, which in many cases is not likely, add the extra middle leaf for more space. Failing that, you will probably have to hunt up a folding dining table or picnic table. In most places these are easy to come by and can be rented quite reasonably.

Once you have the table, the next task is table arrangement. The most important thing to remember here is to pay close attention to planning for your guests' convenience. Care must be taken to balance the table space in terms of serving dishes, place settings, and table decorations.

Take a buffet, for instance. Buffets must be planned such that traffic moves in one direction. That is, guests must be able to take the various dishes comprising the buffet in logical sequence, starting at one end of the table with the dinner plates and main dish. Salads, vegetables, condiments, and appetizers follow in logical order according to their sequence in a meal. Everything is placed, along with the serving pieces, near the edge of the table within easy reach. Silver and serviettes are ideally placed at the opposite end of the table from the main dish or dishes, so they can be picked up last. Beverages, including punch, coffee, bar drinks, should be placed on a separate table to prevent overcrowding at the main table. Failing that, place them opposite the salad, vegetables, rolls, condiments, and spices. A centrepiece consisting of dried or fresh flowers or wheat stalks and cattails is an ideal decoration for the table and can enhance the overall effect.

The English style of serving is ideal for more formal occasions, such as a dinner party. This is when the dishes are served right at the table and the host does the serving. All dinner plates are placed beside the host, as are the serving utensils. With the food within his easy reach, the host carves the meat, serves the vegetables. Only the condiments and appetizers are passed around. If soup is served, it can either be ladled out of a large soup tureen by the host, or served directly at each place setting. Wine can also be served either by the host or by the guests themselves. If by the guests, several bottles of wine should be placed on the table within easy reach of the guests. The number of bottles depends on how many guests are seated at the table. For example, a dinner for twelve would demand three bottles of wine, one placed at each third of the table, and so on. At formal dinners, all main course dishes are cleared from the table before dessert is served.

Seating depends on personal preference at these affairs, but traditionally the host sits at one end of the table and the hostess at the other. Assuming you have a date for the dinner party, she will sit at one end as the hostess. Your other guests, if in couples, should be separated in a random setting. Alternate the men and women wherever possible.

One important thing for bachelors to learn, fundamental to any formal meal, is proper utensil settings for each guest. The two forks, one for main courses and one for salads and/or appetizers, are placed on the left side. The bread plate and butter knife are placed directly above the forks. The napkin is placed to the left of the forks, and the knife is placed to the right of the plate, sharp edge toward the plate, followed by the spoons. The glasses (one for beverage, one for wine) are placed directly above the knife. Salads, either in bowls or in plates, are always to the left of the forks. Soup bowls and appetizer plates are placed on the dinner plates.

For formal occasions, table centrepieces are a valuable extra, enhancing the entire effect. For the ultimate, use freshly cut flowers or a number of well-placed, brightly lit, colourful candles.

Food Quantities for Larger Groups

In serving larger groups of people, quantities of food are important. Without planning quantities, the host often finds himself short of food or long on several dishes, which inevitably results in needless leftovers.

This situation can be remedied easily if the host studies the following rough guide on food quantities. It has been based on a group of twenty people, and if there are less, say ten, then simply divide the quantities proportionally.

Let's start with soups. Based on a cup of soup per person, the host will need approximately ten eight-ounce cans of condensed soup to feed his guests, or two fifty-ounce cans.

Planning salad quantities depends on what kind of salad you are serving. A lettuce salad is usually planned based on four persons per head of lettuce; so five heads would safely serve twenty guests. A potato salad is based on an average serving of four ounces per person; so you would need about ten cups, or roughly three quarts of salad, for the same number of people. Fruit salad would amount to six cups for twenty people, or two quarts, based on an average serving of one-third cup per person.

If you are serving appetizers, such as olives and pickles, you would need approximately one quart to serve twenty people, based on an average serving of three to four olives per person, and one-ounce servings of pickles per person.

Remember that pastas double in cooking. Based on a four-ounce serving per person, cooked, you will need approximately one and one-half pounds of rice to feed twenty people, and two and one-half pounds of spaghetti and noodles, based on an average serving of three-quarters cup cooked.

Meats can be just as easily estimated. For example, if serving a beef chuck roast, based on an average per-person serving of four ounces, you must plan on a twelve- to thirteen-pound roast. With ground beef, based on a four-ounce serving, and allowing for meat shrinkage, twenty people can be fed with about eight pounds of beef. With a baked ham, you will need at least a ten-pound ham for the same number of people. With chicken and turkey, allowing for bones and shrinkage, twenty people can be fed with a ten-pound fowl. Turkey roll, based again on a four-ounce serving per person, will require you to purchase at least a five-to six-pound roll for twenty guests. In fact a high quality turkey roll is in many ways superior to buying a whole turkey or chicken as there is almost no waste. However, leftover meat can be incorporated readily into other dishes; so you may not worry about leftovers here.

Vegetables also take careful planning. Plan on one baked potato per person, or about eight pounds of raw potatoes per twenty people. Mashed potatoes will require you to buy about seven pounds of raw potatoes to serve the same twenty people, again based on four-ounce individual servings. Frozen vegetables such as beans (green or waxed), carrots, corn, and peas, based on an average serving of one-third cup per person, mean you will have to buy about five pounds to serve twenty guests. And if you are planning to serve French fries and are buying frozen French fries at the supermarket, you will need about four pounds to serve twenty comfortably. With canned vegetables, one-half can will serve one nicely, so ten eight-ounce cans will do the trick for twenty, or one six- to seven-pound large can, or two one-pound-twelve-ounce cans.

Desserts are more difficult to estimate. Cake quantities, for instance, depend on the size and kind of cake. But roughly, one wedge of cake per person, five people per cake, or four cakes per twenty-person gathering. If the cake is cut into squares, two 9" x 12" cakes should yield enough squares to feed the same number of people. As for ice cream, three quarts should do for twenty guests, with an average serving of four ounces per person. Pie, if based on an average serving of one-sixth pie per person, means four nine-inch pies every twenty people. And if you are topping your desserts with whipped cream, homemade, buy a single pint of whipping cream for the same twenty guests.

Beverage quantities depend on the time of the year, the amount of the other liquid refreshments, and your guests' tastes. But you can count on two cups of coffee per person, so a pound (five cups) of coffee should cover an evening's coffee drinking with twenty friends. The same goes for tea. A pint of cream for the coffee or tea will do nicely. As for carbonated beverages, count on two people per family-sized bottle for normal mealtime consumption, or one person per family-size bottle if mixed drinks with liquor are being served. If you are having juice, as in apple or tomato juice appetizers, plan on two forty-six-ounce cans for twenty people.

Cooking for crowds, then, is something that you should enjoy and an art you will become proficient at with a little practice. The tips outlined here should be enough to allow you to handle any group of people up to twenty, with ideas for serving, table decoration, even meal suggestions.

Notes

VI

Wine deserves a special place in any cookbook, particularly because of its mystery. Most meals can be enhanced by the addition of a good bottle of wine; therefore bachelors should know something about wine so they can exercise some discretion in its use.

Budget considerations can limit the scope of your wine knowledge. Few of us will ever be able to afford to try the greatest wines in the world, but this does not prevent us from sampling some of the best reasonable wines available on the market today. And often you will find the best of the low cost wines are superb! You may even discover a wine that will someday be a collector's item.

You may have to put yourselves on a wine budget as many European families do, and if wines go up in price, start looking at less expensive wines for a special hidden bargain. In a few months of sampling, you will begin to know which wines are great according to your own personal taste and then you can stock the wines you have come to like.

Sampling is the key to the wine-budget school of thinking forced upon bachelors by the extreme escalation in prices for good wines. Buy half a dozen wines of different types but basically around the same price range within your budget and invite some friends over for a sampling. When you discover something special, hurry back and order more.

Try Spanish reds, German whites, Austrian and Spanish sparkling wines, and do not ignore California wines. Many of the California wines are at par or superior to European wines of good quality because of the more consistent growing season in the American state.

One suggestion for broadening your tastes without going beyond your budget is to purchase great names in off years. You will find that many ultraexpensive wines have neighbours from the same vineyard or the same region which cost substantially less and taste every bit as good, or almost as good. Only a true wine gourmet would be able to taste the difference, but for the general bachelor-gourmet the off-label should do nicely. For example almost anyone familiar with French wines knows about Pouilly-Fuissé, but how many have heard of Pouilly-Vinzelles, an area close to Pouilly-Fuissé that has the same grapes and similar soil, and produces a wine not too far removed in quality from its more famous neighbour.

Once you have had several samplings, whether through a wine-tasting party or through the use of wine with your meals, you will no doubt want to buy several bottles of a wine. Who knows, maybe you will make a new "find" right in your own home.

Once you have reached the stage where you are beginning to think of collecting wines seriously, it may be a good move to make a wine cellar. While younger wines can be stored safely for a few months in any dark and reasonably cool spot, aging for longer periods of time should be done in a place that is free from vibration and can be kept at a constant temperature of around fifty-five to sixty degrees Fahrenheit or 13 to 18 degrees Celsius. There is no reason why you can not fix up an area inexpensively to store wine in a home or apartment. A cellar can be improvised in a closet or even an attic.

Once you have established a wine cellar, you can really start having fun with wines! You will not be disappointed by your new hobby. With your knowledge will come the satisfaction of matching a bottle of good wine with a particular menu at a reasonable price.

Here are several tips on wines and how and when to use them, plus a few names that stand out in each category:

Cork-sniffing has traditionally been required by etiquette, but this practice can be abandoned today, except by the wine connoisseurs. If it is done, it should no longer be reserved for the male, but should be an option open to either male or female guests. If a cork smells particularly sour, or if the cork appears very bouncy and new-looking, it is advisable to overlook the wine completely as it may either be sour or too new for most tastes.

As for what wines to have with what, read on.

Appetizer wines and sherry, vermouth, port, and Dubonnet can be served on the rocks or in wine glasses, slightly chilled. They need no accompaniment, but you may want some light appetizers to go with them.

Red table wines are good with all red meats, game, poultry, and cheese and should be served at room temperature.

White table wines are good with chicken, turkey, in fact, all kinds of poultry, fish and shellfish, and ham. Ask at your local supplier for new white wines on the market that he recommends (this applies to all other wines as well).

Dessert wines are good with fruit, cakes, and dessert cheeses. Port, Dubonnet, and fruit-flavoured wines are ideal and fairly light. They should be served at room temperature.

Sparkling wines, including champagne, are perhaps the most versatile wines and may become your greatest love. They go well with everything and every occasion. There are seemingly countless varieties that will tempt your fancy. The best advice here is to try one from every country, particularly the

Spanish varieties. Eventually you will find several that you will want for more special occasions.

Cheese complements any wines. In the next chapter on entertaining you will find a list of staple cheeses that complement any or all of the wines discussed in this chapter.

Finally, any good wine deserves a great gourmet meal, twelve of which you will find in the last chapter in this book. With that chapter behind you, we will have a true gourmet on our hands before we know it!

Cooking Gourmet

16·X·77 BRACEBRIDGE

VII

Now that your stage fright over the world of cooking is over, perhaps you are ready to get a glimpse of a more advanced kind of meal preparation, gourmet cooking.

By now you have learned how to stock your kitchen cupboards, what utensils to buy, and picked up tips that can save you time and money in your new hobby. Perhaps you have tried one of the informal suggested parties for entertaining large groups of friends, such as a fondue party. It has probably gone well, and you are now ready to try cooking that is even more challenging, cooking a gourmet meal, the true test of any aspiring cook.

You will have to go all out here, because gourmet cooking takes not only a love for good food but careful preparation and attention to every cooking detail. So if you are ready for it, look over this chapter. Aside from briefly discussing the various courses that make up a meal, the chapter gives you twelve menus from which to choose.

Ingredients, preparation, cooking steps, and serving suggestions are all included in each menu; and each menu contains suggestions for a complete meal from start to finish. As these menu suggestions are primarily dinner suggestions, the quantities they yield will safely serve four to six people, focussing on sharpening your cooking skills for small, intimate gatherings.

The reason for having only twelve menus is simple. Most of us are limited as to time and budget, and making one gourmet meal every month seems about as much of gourmet cooking as one can handle. What you have is enough gourmet meal suggestions to last you for an entire year. If that is not enough, then you are really hooked! And, as has been said before *How to Boil Water* is a book intended only to serve you in your early cooking career as a guide and inspiration. If you decide to expand your cooking skills beyond this book, then the book has indeed done its job well. Once you have tried all the menus suggested in this chapter, look at other gourmet books with the author's blessings. That is exactly what was intended!

Care has been taken to suggest complete meals that differ as to country of origin. There are French classics, German favourites, Greek delights, hearty Czechoslovakian food, traditional English meals, and familiar North

American stand-bys. All are relatively challenging. Ones that present the most challenge have a **** designation above them.

Every menu is planned for the maximum in cooking enjoyment and taste experience. After you have prepared them all, the world of cooking should have acquired another lifetime gourmet, ready to try other equally interesting meals from other countries. Those I leave for you to discover. This chapter will only serve to whet your appetite. You will soon develop your own specialities and preferences.

Now on to a brief discussion on the courses that make up a typical gourmet meal.

Appetizers

Although this book will not go into detail on appetizers, they are often a good thing to serve your guests early in the evening. Chicken livers broiled and wrapped in bacon are always good, as are pickles, olives, antipasto, and party wieners. Because the meals suggested here are quite involved in preparation and also very filling, the appetizers have been left to you. Appetizers can be quite filling and perhaps serve only to spoil one's appetite for the true taste experiences awaiting from the meal itself. Others may strongly disagree. If you must, serve only light appetizers such as the ones listed above. They take relatively little preparation and are not too filling. Your cooking energies should instead be devoted to the meal itself.

Soups

Many people forget about making soups and go on to the next course instead. This could be a mistake because soups are fun to make from scratch and can often steal the spotlight away from the main course. Every good meal deserves a great soup, whether is it a clear broth, a creamed classic, or an aristocratic baked onion soup. In fact it can even be a meal in itself, such as the classic French creation, Bouillabaise, which is discussed later in this chapter (Gourmet Menu 12).

Two important soup ingredients are bones and seasonings. Bones add body to soup liquid so it is wise to put soup bones in as often as they are available. Remove them once they have given their flavour to the soup stock. With seasonings you have a chance to experiment. Do not use too many in one soup, but try varying combinations each time. Tabasco sauce, Worcestershire sauce, HP, Chef sauce, soy sauce, Beau Monde, mustard (both dry and vinegar mustard), ketchup, chili powder, Lea and Perrins, barbecue salt, the list is endless.

Herbs, such as oregano, thyme, parsley, chives, cinnamon, and ginger are all welcome additions to a basic soup stock. Even cloves and dill can make a soup something special.

And wines are a natural additive, preferably cooking wines such as sherry and port, but also any leftover whites or reds you may have on hand. Beer can enhance the taste of a hearty beef soup.

Fundamental to any good soup is the basic soup stock. There are two schools of thought here, one truly gourmet and the other more practical. The gourmet school suggests that any and all soups should be made with a basic homemade stock, adding the other ingredients to finish off the soup. This takes a great deal of time and effort but the results are indeed worth it. The more practical school, on the other hand, suggests that making soup stock from scratch is too time-consuming and it is better to purchase prepared canned soup stocks and finish the soup from that point.

Which to choose is up to personal taste and time restrictions, but as far as taste goes the gourmet school of thought will win out over the practical. So for those of you who want to be true food connoisseurs, here are two recipes for making basic soup stock from scratch, one for beef stock, the other for chicken stock. A third stock, fish stock, is dealt with as Court Bouillion in Gourmet Menu 12 of this chapter.

Beef Stock

Approximate preparation and cooking time: 2½ hours

Ingredients:

    1 lb. veal knuckles, coarsely chopped by butcher
    1 lb. beef knuckles, coarsely chopped by butcher
    4 tbsp. cooking fat
    2 lbs. lean beef
    2 chicken feet, if available from butcher
    1 large onion, stuck with 2 whole cloves
    2 leeks, white parts only, if available
    2 stalks celery, tops included
    2 carrots, coarsely chopped
    1 large clove garlic
    Salt, freshly ground black pepper
    3 quarts water

Preparation and cooking steps:

Brown the bones in a frying pan in oil, transfer with the rest of the ingredients and water to a large pot and bring to a boil. Allow to boil for one hour, skimming off the scum rising in the water. Set stove to simmer and cook another hour until meat is tender. Strain the soup through a sieve, cool, and remove as much fat as possible. Use in other recipes, as a soup by itself, or freeze it for later use.

Note: If placed in the refrigerator and kept overnight, the fat will rise to the surface and form a hard crust. Simply remove this crust for pure, fat-free beef stock.

Chicken Stock

Approximate preparation and cooking time: 2½ hours

Ingredients:

1 lb. boiling chicken, cut up
1 lb. veal knuckle, coarsely chopped by butcher
2 leeks, white parts only, if available
1 large onion, stuck with 2 whole cloves
2 coarsely chopped carrots
2 celery stalks, with tops
1 large garlic clove
Parsley, either dried or fresh
Salt, freshly ground black pepper
4 chicken feet, if available from butcher
3 quarts water

Preparation and cooking steps:

Brown the meat and bones and cook in water in large pot for one hour, skimming scum. Then add vegetables and simmer for another hour. Put liquid through a sieve and save stock. Follow the same procedure for fat-free beef stock and for storage.

Salad

Remember that a salad is a perfect, year-round, all-occasion menu picker-upper. And also remember that freshness makes a salad, so take care to select only the best and freshest vegetables for your salad dishes and take time in preparing them. Always chill a salad in the refrigerator before serving as this ensures freshness and crispness.

Vegetables

Again, freshness is important here, so take special care. Colour enhances the meal's effect on your guests, too; so if you are serving a bland looking main course, serve a bright vegetable dish, such as a tomato-based dish, to pick up the colour and visual appeal of the overall meal. A delicately flavoured main dish calls for a low-key vegetable with a subtle taste, so be careful to think of this in your planning as well when it comes to preparing vegetables with a meal.

Beef and Poultry

The first rule of thumb here is to buy what you need when you need it, fresh. Frozen meats are good in a bind or when you are eating day-to-day, but fresh meats and poultry are necessary when cooking gourmet. Secondly, always salt your meat before cooking, and always use freshly-ground black pepper when cooking gourmet for maximum effect and taste.

Fish and Shellfish

Freshness is also essential to fish cookery. Whenever possible try to purchase your fish and shellfish fresh, but if this is not possible, frozen defrosted fish will have to do. When you buy fresh fish, firmness is essential to cooking; always choose a firm fleshed fresh fish, testing it yourself. And be careful, when buying frozen fish, to avoid freezer burned items.

Rice, Potatoes, Pastas, Breads

Learn to appreciate the value of rice and potatoes and pastas as meal-savers, even when cooking gourmet. Rice can be made a million different ways, as can the other two. The addition of a little spice, sauce, or other seasoning or vegetable can turn these meal savers into truly gourmet dishes. In fact an entire book could (and probably has) been written on exactly this subject; so try to seek out recipes that will incorporate these starchy foods into your menus when you get beyond this book. As for breads, the pros of freshly-baked over store-bought are needless to say, many. Suffice it to say that the taste of your own baking can never be beaten.

Desserts

For many people dessert is really what a gourmet meal is all about, something very rich and heavy, something filling. Ideally, however, the dessert should not be too heavy as meal balance is essential in any properly planned menu, including (and especially) gourmet menus.

After a hearty, homemade soup, a good salad, and a tempting main course, not to mention a few drinks and wine, the effect of a heavy dessert is often disastrous to the overall effect of the meal you have spent hours preparing. Then come the "I can't believe I ate the whole thing" complaints, and this you do not deserve. So keeping that in mind, try to prepare something light and fluffy for dessert.

Nevertheless if you are going to give in to the temptations of the rich dessert, and they are indeed tempting, try to save the dessert for later in the evening so the other courses can be partially digested before topping them off in your stomachs with a crunchingly rich dessert!

Sauces

It is good to know something about the preparation of a number of sauces that can be used with main courses and as desserts.

Sweet Sauces

The sweet sauces are all derivatives of a basic *crème à l'anglaise* sauce which is a form of egg custard. To make the basic sauce (*crème à l'anglaise*), scald eight ounces of milk and eight ounces of cream with one teaspoon vanilla extract mixed with two teaspoons cornstarch, four eggs and two ounces sugar over a pan of piping hot water. Stir constantly, taking care never to allow it to reach a boil. When it is thick and creamy, it is ready.

If you add a teaspoon of gelatin mixed with a little water into this, you will have an excellent glaze called *crème à l'anglaise Collée*.

If you want a filling for pastries and cakes, heat your *crème à l'anglaise* to lukewarm and beat in one-half pound of unsalted butter, a spoonful at a time.

And if you want a mousse-like dessert, make your *crème à l'anglaise* using eight eggs instead of the usual four, add some gelatin and water; or cool *crème à l'anglaise Collée*, and fold in four well-beaten egg whites and a half pint of heavy whipping cream. Refrigerate in a heavy mold, turn out, and serve as a great dessert. It's called *crème Bavaroise*.

Note also that you may flavour any or all of the above cream sauces by adding a couple of ounces of melted baking chocolate, some strong coffee (like espresso), or a brandy or liqueur. There are many variations on the same basic theme.

Meat and Fish Sauces

Many sauces have a base made of a rich brown stock. To save time why not use some of the basic beef stock we talked about early in the chapter and boil it down. Take two cups of basic beef stock, simmer it in a saucepan for a half hour or so, until it is reduced by half. You will have a thick dark liquid, very concentrated. This is called *glacé de viande*, or meat extract, and is a great sauce for meat. In other words, it can be used as a basic building stock which, when added to, creates useful meat sauces.

Similarly a basic white stock can be made using a basic chicken stock and reducing its volume correspondingly in half as with beef stock.

Once a white stock is made, use it for making a *velouté*, a white cream sauce perfect as a base for other white sauces. To make *velouté*, stir two ounces of butter and two of flour over low heat in a saucepan to make a *roux* and then add one pint of the hot white stock slowly while stirring. This *velouté* will form the base of Sauce Supreme, perfect for chicken and lamb, when a quarter pint of warm cream is added to the *velouté*.

For a Béchamel sauce, add one pint of hot milk instead of white stock, using the *velouté* recipe.

For a Soubise sauce, served with lamb or vegetables, add a pound of chopped onion, cooked soft, and a half pint of white wine to a pint of the Béchamel sauce. And for Mornay sauce, which is great on eggs, fish, veal, poultry and vegetables, add six ounces grated cheese to a pint of Béchamel and heat.

Hollandaise sauce, delicious with fish, is made using a heat proof bowl and stirring into it three raw egg yolks, one tablespoon lemon juice, and six ounces butter cut into pea-sized cubes. Do this over a pan of boiling water for maximum results. Serve it warm over a hot fish dish, and for even more flavouring in the sauce, vary the lemon juice with homemade fish stock instead.

Béarnaise sauce is made with two ounces dry white wine, two ounces vinegar, one tablespoon chopped onion and one tablespoon chopped tarragon, heated and strained, and added to a basic Hollandaise sauce. For an even richer fish sauce, make a mousseline sauce, using one-quarter pint cream beaten thick, folded into three-quarters pint Béarnaise sauce just before you serve it.

Another variation is to make a Béarnaise sauce and stir into a mixture of a tablespoon of *glacé de viande* and two tablespoons dry white wine, heated for five minutes.

Again using the Béarnaise sauce, try adding six ounces of tomato paste to one point of the Béarnaise for steak, chicken, fish and egg dishes. It's called Choron sauce.

Now that you have that behind you, you are ready to read on to find out what menu suggestions await your cooking talents. There are twelve to choose from, one for each month of this year; so take your pick in whatever order you wish. Some are more difficult than others. You will be able to tell them by the **** designation. Good luck!

1

Cheese Loaf and Sour Cream
Lancashire Hot Pot
Peas and Carrots
Tea

Approximate preparation and cooking time: 2 hours

Ingredients:

1. Cheese Loaf

½ cup butter, soft
¼ cup sugar
3 eggs
¾ cup milk
1¼ cups flour
1 tsp. baking powder
½ tsp. salt
1 lb. dry cottage cheese
1 pint sour cream

2. Hot Pot

6 shoulder lamb chops
6 large potatoes
Salt, pepper
6 lamb kidneys
6 oysters, fresh or canned
¼ lb. mushrooms, same
1 large onion, diced

3. Peas and Carrots

Short cut here:
2 8-oz. cans

Preparation and cooking steps:

1. Preheat oven to 350 degrees.

2. *Hot Pot:* Peel potatoes and cut them into half-inch cubes. Spread about one-third of the potatoes on bottom of a greased four- to five-quart ovenproof casserole and put three lamb chops (all trimmed of fat) side by side on top. Sprinkle with salt and pepper and cover with three lamb kidneys (first removing the membranes and dicing them), three oysters, one-quarter pound mushrooms, and diced onion. Cover with another one-third potatoes, then put the other three lamb chops on the potatoes and top that with the next three oysters and lamb kidneys. Cover with remaining potatoes. Cover the whole thing with water, place covered casserole in oven for one and one-half hours. Remove cover, bake a further half hour, serve immediately.

3. *Cheese Loaf:* Cream butter and sugar. Add two eggs, milk, and flour with baking powder, and salt, until blended into smooth batter. Pour half batter into a greased baking pan. Then mix dry cottage cheese, one egg, a pinch of salt and sugar, and pour onto the batter in the pan. Pour the remaining

batter over the cheese mixture and heat for forty-five minutes until brown. Cook during the final stages of the hot pot dish.

4. *Peas and Carrots:* Open cans, drain and heat vegetables. Serve with hot pot.

5. Serve Cheese Loaf as dessert with sour cream. Accompany with tea as beverage. Serve after an interval of one hour after main course has been eaten.

2 American

Mexican Fiesta Salad
Stuffed Breast of Chicken
Pineapple Upside Down Cake
White Wine
Coffee

Preparation and cooking time: 1½ hours

Ingredients:

1. Salad

4 slices bacon
1 head lettuce
1 large avocado
1 green pepper
4 tomatoes
1 small onion
1½ tsp. chili powder
½ tsp. salt
⅓ cup cider vinegar

3. Cake

¼ cup brown sugar
¼ cup margarine
1 lb. sliced canned pineapple
3 eggs
1 cup granulated sugar
1 cup flour
1 tsp. baking soda
¼ tsp. salt

2. Chicken

4 large chicken breasts
1 can mushrooms (or fresh)
¼ cup celery, finely chopped
Parsley, fresh or dried
1 small onion
Flour
Salt, pepper
1 can condensed onion soup
Soy sauce

Preparation and cooking steps:

1. Preheat oven to 350 degrees.

2. *Salad:* Fry bacon in small saucepan until crisp, save fat, and set aside. Peel and pit the avocado, peel and dice the tomatoes, seed and chop the green pepper, chop onion, tear the lettuce finely. Arrange the lettuce around a salad bowl and slice the avocado, arranging the slices around the edge of the bowl like flower petals. Throw the diced tomatoes into the bowl, sprinkle with the green pepper and onion, and crumble the cooked bacon into it. Stir the chili powder and salt into the bacon drippings, add the cider vinegar, heat and pour over the salad. Serve from the large bowl right at the table.

3. *Chicken:* Bone the chicken breasts. Slit the thick portion of each breast to form a pocket. In a large frying pan, cook fresh or canned mushrooms that you have chopped finely, celery, and a tablespoon of fresh parsley (or one-half tablespoon chopped dried parsley), with one-quarter cup finely chopped onions until tender. Spoon mixture into the pockets and pinch edges of pockets to seal. Coat the chicken breasts with flour, salt and pepper them, brown in oil in a hot frying pan and put them into a baking dish. Then insert dish into the oven for forty-five minutes, or until chicken is tender. Baste periodically with a can of onion soup mixed with some soy sauce. Serve when ready with slightly chilled white wine.

4. *Cake:* Slowly cook brown sugar and margarine in a small saucepan. Drain and add sliced pineapple, reserving the juice. Cook and cool and line the bottom of a 9- or 10-inch cake pan. Next, beat eggs together with a cup of granulated sugar until mixture is light and fluffy, and add one-half cup of the reserved pineapple juice. Mix separately, flour, baking soda, and salt. Combine with egg mixture and pour over the pineapples. Bake for three-quarters of an hour at 350 degrees, uncovered. Turn out upside down onto a serving plate. Serve with hot coffee.

****

3 German

Borsch
Sauerbraten
Potato Pancakes with Applesauce
Beer

Approximate preparation and cooking time: a) marinating—3 days
b) cooking—2½ hours

Ingredients:

1. Borsch

4 medium tomatoes
4 tbsp. butter
1 cup minced onion
2 cloves garlic
1 lb. beets
1 stalk celery, sliced
1 grated parsnip root
½ tsp. sugar
¼ cup red wine vinegar
1 tbsp. salt
Dried parsley
2 quarts beef stock
  (fresh or canned)
1 lb. potatoes, diced
1 lb. cabbage, shredded
1 lb. beef brisket

b) Meat
5 lbs. boneless roast
½ cup chopped onions
½ cup chopped carrots
½ cup chopped celery
1 pinch powdered ginger

3. Pancakes

6 medium potatoes
2 eggs
¼ cup minced onion
⅓ cup flour
1 tsp. salt
Lard or cooking oil
1 8-oz. can prepared applesauce,
  optional

2. Sauerbraten

a) Marinade
   ½ cup dry red wine
   ½ cup red wine vinegar
   2 cups water
   1 medium onion, thinly sliced
   6 crushed peppercorns

Preparation and cooking steps:

Note: Marinating meat begins three days prior to cooking, so plan
accordingly.

1. *Marinade:* Combine red wine, wine vinegar, water, crushed peppercorns,

and onion. Heat to a boil in a saucepan and allow to cool. Place the roast in an ovenproof enamel pot (five-quart capacity), and pour the marinade over it. Allow to marinate for three days in the refrigerator, turning the meat at least twice a day (before you go to work and when you come home). Then dry off the meat the day of cooking with paper towels, strain the marinade and save the liquid.

2. *Cooking the Meat:* Brown the meat on all sides in the same casserole for fifteen minutes in lard or cooking oil. Remove the meat and cook the onions, carrots, and celery for five minutes at medium heat in the casserole. Pour in two cups of the marinade and one-half cup water and bring to a boil. Remove the liquid from the casserole, replace the roast, and cook the roast in the oven for one and a half hours at 350 degrees, or until meat is cooked rare. While the meat cooks, take the liquid you have reserved, add a pinch of ginger powder, and cook for about ten minutes in a saucepan. When the meat is cooked, strain the cooked liquid, slice the meat in thin slices, and pour the cooked marinade over it. Serve piping hot with the potato pancakes.

3. *Borsch:* While the meat is browning, boil four medium tomatoes for fifteen seconds in boiling water and peel the skins.. Remove the seeds and core, chop finely and set aside. Fry the onions and garlic (crushed) for five to ten minutes or until soft. Stir into them the beets, celery, and parsnip, with half the tomatoes, the sugar, vinegar, salt, a bit of parsley and one and one-half cups of beef stock, either prepared or homemade. Bring to a boil, cover and simmer for forty minutes. Meanwhile, pour remaining beef stock into a large pot, add the diced potatoes and shredded cabbage, and boil until the potatoes are tender. Add the vegetable mixture, the remaining tomatoes and seeds and core, and the piece of beef brisket. Cook for another forty minutes and serve before the Sauerbraten is done, if possible with some freshly baked store-bought rye bread.

Note: If preparing beef stock from scratch for this recipe, add a further one and a half hours to the preparation time. Perhaps, though, you will want to use prepared beef stock instead, as the rest of the menu is complicated enough to want to avoid making beef stock.

4. *Pancakes:* While the soup and meat cook, grate potatoes coarsely into a sieve and squeeze out all the moisture possible. Stir the potatoes into a mixture of beaten eggs, onion, salt, and flour, and beat together in a large bowl. Preheat electric frying pan or saucepan and melt lard or fat until it sputters. Shape the potato mixture into balls and fry as you would pancakes over high heat until brown on both sides. Wrap in foil and set aside in the prewarmed oven where the meat is cooking. When the meat is done, serve hot with the meat as a side dish. Top each serving of pancakes with applesauce if desired.

4 American

Herbed Chicken
Pineapple-Ham Salad
Devilled Brussels Sprouts
Pecan Pie
Coffee

Approximate preparation and cooking time: 2 hours

Ingredients:

1. Chicken

   4 chicken breasts, boned
   3 oz. white rice
   3 oz. wild rice
   1 10½ oz. can condensed
       cream of chicken soup
   ¾ cup sauterne wine
   ½ cup sliced celery
   ½ cup sliced mushrooms
   ½ small can pimentos, chopped
       fine
   1 medium onion, minced

2. Salad
   1 head lettuce
   2 cups cooked ham, diced
   1 large can pineapple chunks
   Mayonnaise
   Pepper
   Prepared mustard
   Sweet pickle relish
   Prepared horseradish
   1 diced green pepper

3. Vegetables

   2 lbs. Brussels sprouts
   Prepared mustard
   Worcestershire sauce
   Chili sauce, prepared
   Salt, pepper
   Butter or margarine

4. Pie

   1 9-inch pie crust, baked
   2 eggs, separated
   ½ cup brown sugar
   Salt, cinnamon, vanilla
   1 cup dark corn syrup
   1 tbsp. flour
   ¾ cup coarsely chopped pecans
   ¼ cup whole pecans
   ½ cup butter or margarine,
       melted
   Whipping cream, optional

Preparation and cooking steps:

1. *Chicken:* Prepare rice as you normally would (takes about 20 minutes). Drain and set aside. Season the chicken and brown it in butter in large frying pan. Spoon the rice into a one and one-half quart ovenproof casserole, top with the chicken, skin side up. Combine condensed cream of chicken soup with sauterne wine in a skillet, bring to a boil, and add celery, mushrooms, pimentos, and onion. Cook for five minutes and pour over the chicken in the casserole. Cover and bake at 350 degrees for at least thirty minutes.

102

2. *Pie:*
   a) Bake your pie shell (a prepared pie shell will do) for about twenty minutes or until golden brown in the prewarmed oven while the chicken is cooking.
   b) Beat two egg yolks, add brown sugar, a pinch of salt, a half teaspoon cinnamon, flour, melted butter or margarine, ½ tsp. vanilla, and corn syrup, and beat well. Then beat two egg whites until stiff and fold them into the egg yolk mixture, adding chopped pecans. Pour into baked pie shell and bake for forty-five minutes at 350 degrees. Cool. Top with whole pecans, arranged decoratively, and perhaps with some whipped cream.

3. *Vegetables:* While chicken cooks, boil fresh or frozen Brussels sprouts in salted water for fifteen minutes and drain. Then melt some butter or margarine in a large saucepan, add two teaspoons prepared mustard, one teaspoon Worcestershire sauce, one tablespoon chili sauce, and salt and pepper to taste. Pour this over the Brussels sprouts once it has simmered and is smooth (about five minutes) and serve with the chicken hot from the oven.

4. *Salad:* While Brussels sprouts are boiling, tear lettuce into pieces and line a large salad bowl with them. Put diced ham in centre. Arrange drained pineapple chunks around ham. Blend diced green pepper, one fourth cup mayonnaise, one teaspoon prepared mustard and two tablespoons sweet relish with one tablespoon prepared horseradish and toss with the ham and pineapple. Serve with chicken and vegetables.

5 ****
Italian

Chicken Cacciatore
Italian Appetizer Salad
Stuffed Zucchini
Minestrone Soup
Spumoni Ice Cream
Espresso

Approximate preparation and cooking time: 2½ hours

Ingredients:

1. Chicken

    4 lbs. chicken, cut up
    Flour
    2 cloves garlic, mashed
    2 medium onions, diced
    1 can prepared tomatoes
        (1 lb. 12 oz.)
    1 green pepper
    1 small can pimentos, chopped
    Oregano, thyme
    Salt, pepper, one bay leaf,
        dried parsley
    ⅔ cup dry red wine
    8 oz. can tomato juice
    2 cups sliced mushrooms,
        fresh or canned (drained)
    8 oz. raw spaghetti (No. 9)

2. Salad

    1 cauliflower, broken into
        flowerets
    1 head red lettuce
    1 can cut green beans (1 lb.)
    1 can red kidney beans (1 lb.)
    1 can garbanzo beans (1 lb.)
    3 green onions, chopped
    6 hard-cooked eggs, sliced
    1 cup olive oil
    ½ cup vinegar
    1½ tsp. salt, pepper to taste
    1 can pitted black olives, sliced
    2 sliced tomatoes
    Anchovies

3. Vegetables

    2 lbs. zucchini, fresh or canned
    2 eggs
    ⅓ cup bread crumbs
    ⅓ cup grated Parmesan cheese
    ¼ cup salad oil
    1 minced onion
    Salt, pepper
    Garlic salt
    Parsley
    Thyme

4. Soup

    ½ cup dry white beans
    4 tbsp. butter
    1 cup canned peas, drained
    1 cup diced zucchini
    2 carrots, sliced
    1 cup diced potatoes
    ⅓ cup diced celery
    2 oz. salt pork, minced
    2 tbsp. chopped onion
    1 can tomatoes (1 lb. 12 oz),
        chopped
    2 quarts chicken stock,
        homemade or canned
    1 tsp. dried parsley
    1 bay leaf
    Salt, freshly ground black
        pepper to taste
    ½ cup dry white rice

Preparation and cooking steps:

1. *Soup:* Boil a quart of water in a four- to five-quart casserole, add the white beans, boil a couple of minutes, then reduce heat and cook for one and a half hours until they are barely tender. Drain and set the beans aside. Then cook the peas, zucchini, carrots, potatoes, and celery in butter in a casserole on top of stove for five minutes, stirring constantly so they do not brown. Set them aside. Cook the onion in cooking oil with the minced salt pork for five minutes. Stir in the tomatoes and the vegetables, the chicken stock, the bay leaf, parsley, salt, and pepper. Bring to a boil and simmer for twenty-five minutes. Remove the bay leaf and add the rice and beans, and cook at least another twenty-five minutes. Serve just before the chicken is ready to eat.

2. *Chicken:* Dredge the chicken with flour and brown it in a frying pan in oil. Remove. Then sauté garlic and onions in the hot chicken fat. Add tomatoes, a thinly sliced green pepper, and two tablespoons of chopped pimento and a half teaspoon dried parsley. Add some salt, a pinch of thyme, some oregano, pepper, bay leaf, dry red wine, and tomato juice. Cover this and simmer for forty-five minutes until tender. Add fresh mushrooms, thinly sliced, and cover again. Cook another fifteen minutes.

3. *Spaghetti:* Add dry spaghetti to a quart of boiling salted water and cook for fifteen minutes or until spaghetti is tender. Drain and set aside. Do this while chicken simmers.

4. *Salad:* While chicken simmers, parboil the cauliflower in boiling salted water (can be the same water as the spaghetti cooked or cooks in), and drain when it is tender (about ten to fifteen minutes). Combine the cauliflower in a large salad bowl with the lettuce, beans, onions, and four of the sliced eggs. Make a dressing out of oil, vinegar, salt, and pepper, mixing them together. Combine the dressing with the vegetables. Garnish with the tomato slices, the remaining sliced eggs, olives, and anchovies. Chill before serving.

5. *Vegetables:* Parboil the zucchini in boiling salted water for fifteen minutes, also while chicken simmers. Drain, trim the ends, and cut into halves lengthwise, carefully digging out the pulp. Lay the shells in a greased, shallow baking dish. Mix together in a bowl eggs, bread crumbs, grated Parmesan cheese, salad oil, minced onion, some parsley, salt, garlic salt, pepper, and thyme to taste. Spoon the mixture into the zucchini shells and bake for thirty minutes or until golden brown.

6. *Serving:* Remove the chicken from the oven when tender. Place the spaghetti on a large serving platter; spoon the liquid from the chicken over the spaghetti. Then arrange the chicken on the spaghetti and sauce. Place the cooked zucchini around the edges. Serve the salad in a large bowl.

7. *Dessert:* Serve commercial spumoni ice cream with hot instant espresso as a complementary beverage. If you feel really ambitious, purchase an espresso maker and grind and prepare your own espresso.

6 American

Barbecued Spareribs
Marinated Bean Salad
Oven-baked "French Fried" Potatoes
Lime Pie
Coffee

Approximate preparation and cooking time: a) 6 hours marinating
b) 2½ hours cooking

Ingredients:

1. Spareribs

    3 lbs. baby back pork ribs,
        very lean
    ½ cup soy sauce
    2 tbsp. honey
    2 tbsp. vinegar
    1 tsp. cooking sherry
    1 tbsp. garlic, finely chopped
    1 tsp. sugar
    1 can prepared plum sauce
    1 tsp. Worcestershire sauce
    1 tsp. Tabasco sauce

2. Salad

    1 can (1 lb.) red kidney beans, drained
    1 can garbanzo beans, (1 lb.) drained
    1 can black-eyed peas, (1 lb.) drained
    2½ cups chopped celery
    1 bunch green onions, chopped
    1 small jar stuffed green olives
    1 can pitted black olives, chopped
    ½ cup salad oil
    ½ cup red wine vinegar
    Salt, pepper to taste
    2 tsp. brown sugar
    1 minced garlic clove

3. Potatoes

    6 potatoes
    Barbecue salt
    Oil

4. Pie

    1 prepared pie shell, baked
    5 eggs
    1 can (14 oz.) condensed milk
    ¾ cup fresh lime juice
        (9 - 12 limes)
    Whipped cream, optional

Preparation and cooking steps:

1. *Ribs:*
   a) Marinating: Make a marinade for the ribs of soy sauce, honey, vinegar,
      cooking sherry, chopped garlic, sugar, Worcestershire sauce, Tabasco

sauce, and plum sauce. Marinate the ribs for six full hours in the refrigerator before cooking, basting every two hours.

b) Cooking: Preheat oven to 375 degrees. Skewer the ribs to make an S-shaped roasting surface on the meat. Cook the marinated ribs in a roasting pan. Roast this way for forty-five minutes, then raise the heat another fifty degrees to 425 and roast another half hour until golden brown, basting every fifteen minutes with marinade.

2. *Potatoes:* While the ribs are beginning to cook, peel potatoes and cut into 1-inch by 4-inch chunks. Coat with barbecue salt and oil and place on baking sheet. Bake for thirty-five minutes, or until they are golden brown, turning them every so often to prevent sticking.

3. *Salad:* While ribs are marinating, prepare the marinade and vegetables for this salad. For this marinade, you will need salad oil, red wine vinegar, brown sugar, salt and pepper, and a minced clove of garlic. Mix thoroughly and add the beans, peas, celery, green onions, green olives, and black olives. Let stand in the marinade for five to six hours. Serve with the hot ribs and potatoes.

4. *Pie:* Separate egg yolks from whites. Beat five egg yolks until they are thick. Beat in condensed milk and lime juice. Separately, beat the egg whites until they begin to form peaks, but not until stiff. Fold them gently into the other mixture, and spoon into a baked pie shell. Bake in the oven at least twenty minutes and cool in the refrigerator while you are eating the main courses. You may serve this topped with canned or fresh whipped cream.

7 Russian

****

Onion Soup
Baked Apples with Honeyed Applesauce
Caesar Salad
Roast Suckling Pig
Bananas Flambé
White Wine

Approximate preparation and cooking time: 4 hours

Ingredients:

1. Soup

    2½ pints beef stock, either
        homemade or 6 cans (8 oz.)
        prepared
    6 medium onions
    3 tablespoons butter
    3 tablespoons olive oil
    3 tbsp. sugar
    6 tbsp. cognac
    1½ tbsp. wine vinegar
    Mustard (Dijon)
    Salt, freshly ground black pepper
    6 slices toasted French bread
    1 cup grated Gruyère cheese
    Note: You will need 6 soup
        tureens (ovenproof)

2. Apples

    6 red apples
    6 oz. honey
    1 8-oz. can applesauce

3. Salad

    2 raw eggs
    1 clove garlic
    ¾ cup olive oil
    2 large heads romaine lettuce
    ½ tsp. salt
    Freshly ground black pepper
    1 large lemon

    6 - 8 anchovy fillets,
        chopped or minced
    Parmesan cheese, grated
    2 cups prepared croutons

4. Pig

    1 10- to 12-pound suckling pig,
        quartered, the head removed
    Oil
    Salt, pepper
    2 cups rice
    1 apple

5. Bananas

    2 tbsp. butter or margarine
    ½ cup sugar
    ½ cup port wine
    ½ cup red currant jelly
    ½ lemon
    4 bananas
    4 slices drained, canned
        pineapple
    1 large can (1 lb.) Mandarin
        oranges, drained
    ¼ to ½ cup brandy

    Note: You will need a copper-
        bottomed chafing dish.

108

Preparation and cooking steps:

1. *Soup:* Peel and slice the onions very thinly. Heat the olive oil and butter in a large saucepan or electric frying pan, add the onions and cook very, very gently over a low heat, stirring constantly with a wooden spoon until the onions are a golden brown (about twenty-five minutes). Add the beef stock gradually, stir until it begins to boil. Then lower heat, cover, and simmer for an hour. Stir in the cognac, vinegar, and mustard, pour into ovenproof soup tureens. Toast French bread, first cutting into rounds that will fit into the soup tureens. Put the rounds over the individual portions of soup and heap equal portions of grated Gruyère cheese over the bread. Set aside and put into the oven just before the suckling pig is done.

2. *Pig:*
    a) Preheat oven to 375 degrees.
    b) Wash the quartered parts and the head of pig in cold running water. Throw salt and freshly ground black pepper over all the surfaces and coat head and body with vegetable oil. Stuff a ball of aluminum foil into the pig's mouth and cover the pig's ears with foil. Arrange the pig on a rack in a roasting pan as if he were whole and crouching down. Roast for three and a half hours, or about eighteen minutes per pound, until the skin is crisp and the flesh tender. While the pig roasts, boil rice in boiling salted water and drain when done (about twenty minutes). Keep warm. When pig is cooked, remove from oven, take foil ball from mouth and replace it with a fresh, polished red apple. Remove foil from ears. Pour rice onto large serving platter. Place pig on the rice and serve at tableside, carving portions as desired.

3. *Salad:* Crush the garlic clove in a bowl and pour the oil over it. Tear the romaine lettuce into a large salad bowl, sprinkle with salt and pepper, and pour the garlic oil you have just made over it, toss until all the leaves are glossy. Break raw eggs into the lettuce, squeeze in the juice of the lemon, and toss. Add the chopped anchovies (or minced if you prefer a finer sauce) and grated cheese and toss again. Chill in the refrigerator until soup has been served and is finished. Then, bring to table in a large bowl, first adding croutons as a garnish, and serve.

4. *Apples:* Pit and core apples, peel, and cut off the top third of each apple. Into the hole in the centre of each apple, pour equal portions of honey and prepared applesauce. Bake with pig in the same roasting pan, the last twenty minutes that the pig is cooking. To serve, arrange around the serving plate on which the pig rests atop the cooked rice.

5. *Bananas:* Melt butter or margarine in the copper-bottomed chafing dish. Add sugar, port wine, red currant jelly, lemon (grated rind and juice) and stir until mixture is blended. Add peeled sliced bananas, drained canned pineapple, Mandarin oranges, and simmer for about five minutes, tossing the

mixture around until it is all coated with the wine mixture. Then just before serving, heat brandy and pour it over the fruits. Bring it to the table and light it, being very careful to shield yourself and your guests from the flame. To be safe wear an oven mitt on the hand holding the dish or else have it resting on the chafing stand, with the flame underneath. Before lighting, but once you have got it to the table, close the lights in the room for maximum effect.

****

8 Greek

Moussaka
Onion Salad with Feta Cheese
Baklava
Turkish Coffee

Approximate preparation and cooking time: 2½ hours

Ingredients:

1. Moussaka

   1 lb. ground or diced cooked lamb
   1 lb. ham, cooked
   3 tomatoes
   2 large eggplants
   3 garlic cloves
   1 large onion
   1 cup mushrooms, fresh or
      canned
   Salt, pepper, garlic salt
   1 oz. breadcrumbs
   ¼ cup grated cheese
   1 tbsp. lemon peel
   1 8-oz. can beef stock
   1 can tomato paste
   Saffron

2. Salad

   2 small onions
   1 can pimentos
   2 tomatoes
   Oil
   Vinegar
   2 oz. chives
   ½ cup feta cheese
   Pitted black olives

3. Baklava

   1 lb. clarified butter
   ½ cup vegetable oil
   40 16-inch sheets of filo pastry
   ½ cup shelled walnuts, minced
   1½ cups sugar
   ¾ cup water
   1 tbsp. fresh lemon juice
   6 oz. honey
   Note: You will need a large
      baking dish (13" x 9" x 2½")

Preparation and cooking steps:

1. *Baklava:* Clarify a pound of butter by melting it slowly without browning over low heat and skimming off the rising foam. Then let it cool for a few minutes and spoon off the clear butter, leaving the solids at the bottom which you can discard. Preheat the oven to 350 degrees and stir vegetable oil into the clarified butter. Coat a large baking dish with some of the mixture.

Take out forty sheets of filo pastry. (You should be able to find filo pastry at either an Italian or Greek grocery store.) With it before you, fold a sheet of it in half, crosswise, lift it gently and unfold it into the prepared baking dish. Each of the filo sheets should ideally measure 16 x 12 inches. Press the sheet down flat in the dish and brush the whole surface with butter and oil mixture, laying another sheet on top in similar fashion. Then sprinkle the sheet with three tablespoons well-ground walnuts, preferably put through a nut grinder, and repeat the whole procedure (a layer of pastry, a coat of butter and oil, a layer of pastry, walnuts) to make about twenty layers in all. Bake in the oven for thirty minutes, then reduce the heat to 300 degrees and bake another forty-five minutes until crisp and golden. While it is baking, make a syrup of sugar, water, fresh lemon juice, and half of the honey. Heat the syrup to boiling and cook a further five minutes. Stir in the rest of the honey and set it aside. Once you have baked the Baklava, pour the syrup over it and cool to room temperature. Serve in squares. Store the remainder in the refrigerator as a late-evening snack. It will keep for several days.

2. *Moussaka:* If you have bought a precooked ham, cut off what you need and freeze the rest, or cook a raw slice in the oven for ten minutes or until done. Skin and slice the tomatoes. (Skinning is easy if you immerse the tomatoes in boiling, salted water for fifteen seconds and then peel.) Next peel the skin from the eggplants so you have long thin strips of skin left. Save them. Squash the garlic, slice the onion and mushrooms, grate the cheese and mix with the lemon peel and breadcrumbs. Then put the eggplant in boiling water (the same used for the tomatoes) for a few minutes, remove, and dice it into cubes. Line an ovenproof casserole with eggplant skins, fry the eggplant cubes with the onion, garlic, and mushroom mixture in butter in a large frying pan and season to taste with garlic salt, salt, and pepper. Sprinkle the breadcrumbs on the eggplant skins in the dish, then add half of the cooked lamb and the same amount of the ham, cut into small pieces. Add half the cooked vegetables, then a layer of sliced tomatoes. Add the rest of the vegetables, the rest of the lamb, the ham cubes, and more tomatoes. Mix together and add the beef stock, either prepared or homemade, tomato paste, and a pinch of saffron, and pour over casserole. Bake in the oven for twenty minutes at 350 degrees. To serve, invert casserole on a large platter.

3. *Salad:* While the Moussaka is baking, slice onions very thinly, dice half a can of pimentos (freeze the rest for future use), cut tomatoes into thick chunks, and make a dressing out of equal parts of oil and vinegar (preferably olive oil). Toss the salad in the dressing in a large bowl. Sprinkle with feta cheese and olives and chill until ready to serve with the rest of the meal.

4. *Coffee:* Look for Turkish coffee, preferably instant, at your Greek or Italian grocery store. If unavailable, use espresso instant instead. Serve in small cups with Baklava as dessert.

112

9 Czechoslovakian

Szegedin Goulash
Dumplings
Sauerkraut
Honey Cake
Tea

Approximate preparation and cooking time: 4 hours

Ingredients:

1. Goulash

   2 lbs. pork
   3 medium onions
   2 tbsp. lard
   2 tsp. paprika
   1 cup cream
   2 tbsp. flour
   1 quart prepared sauerkraut
       (1 lb. can)

2. Dumplings

   1 lb. flour
   2 eggs
   Salt
   8 slices bread, dried and cubed
   ½ cup milk
   1 oz. yeast

3. Honey cake

   1 cup honey
   ¾ cup oil
   1 cup sugar
   8 eggs
   2½ cups flour
   1 tsp. vanilla
   1 tsp. salt
   1 tsp. soda
   Note: You will need one
   spring-form cake pan.

Preparation and cooking steps:

1. *Dumplings:* In a large bowl, mix flour, eggs, a pinch of salt, bread, milk, and yeast. Set mixture aside, cover, and allow to rise until double in bulk in a warm place or suspended in a larger bowl filled with warm water. When the dough has risen, place it on a well-floured board, divide and shape the dough into a roll and allow it to rise again for about fifteen minutes. Boil some water in a large pot and when the dough has risen again, plunge the roll into the boiling water, cover tightly and continue boiling for a half hour. Insert a mixing spoon into the pot occasionally to keep the roll from sticking to the bottom of the pot. When done, lift from the pot onto a large platter and slice into two-inch-thick portions with a piece of thread.

2. *Goulash:* While the dumplings are rising, fry onions, sliced thinly, in lard

and add paprika. Cover and stew slowly in frying pan, adding pork cut into two-inch cubes. Cook in this manner for forty-five minutes or until the pork is tender. Then add cream and thicken with flour. Add sauerkraut and cook ten minutes longer, stirring occasionally. Serve hot with the dumplings and pour the gravy from the meat over the dumplings as a garnish.

3. *Honey Cake:* Preheat oven to 300 degrees. Boil honey in a saucepan. In a separate bowl, cream oil and sugar together until smooth. Separate eggs; set aside the egg whites. Add egg yolks to the oil and sugar mixture, one at a time mixing thoroughly each time. Add the boiled honey to the egg yolk, oil, sugar mixture, mix well, and then add flour, vanilla, salt, and soda and mix together. Beat the egg whites in a bowl until stiff and fold them gently into the other ingredients in a large mixing bowl. Grease the spring-form pan thoroughly and pour the mixture into it. Bake in the oven for about one hour and fifteen minutes or until the cake springs back to the touch. Cool and remove from pan. Serve with tea.

 **10** French

Roast Duck in Orange Sauce
Wild Rice and Mushrooms
Caesar Salad
Onion Soup
Garlic Bread
Chocolate Mousse

Approximate preparation and cooking time: a) Mousse: 6 hours refrigeration
b) Menu: 3 hours

Ingredients:

1. Duck

   1 5- to 6-lb. duck fresh or frozen,
      defrosted*
   Flour
   2 oranges
   1 tsp. cinnamon
   1 cup dry wine
   ¼ tsp. nutmeg
   1 tbsp. cornstarch
   ½ cup honey
   2 oz. Cointreau, or cognac

2. Rice

   8 oz. wild rice, raw
   6 large fresh mushrooms
   ½ cup Cointreau
   Pan drippings from cooking duck

3. Caesar Salad

   See Gourmet Menu 7

4. Onion Soup

   See Gourmet Menu 7

5. Bread

   1 loaf fresh French bread
   2 cloves garlic
   ½ cup butter

6. Mousse

   4 eggs, separated
   ¼ cup superfine sugar
   3 tbsp. cognac
   6 oz. baking chocolate, sweet
      or semi-sweet
   3 tbsp. espresso instant coffee
   ¼ lb. softened unsalted butter
   1 pint whipping cream
   1 cup superfine sugar
   Ice water

   Note: You will need a fancy bread
      basket, a basting brush, and a
      one-quart charlotte or ring mold

Preparation and cooking steps:

1. *Mousse:*
   a) Begin preparation a six full hours before preparation of rest of the meal.
   b) Coat charlotte or ring mold with a film of vegetable oil and set on paper towels. Then beat egg yolks and a quarter-cup superfine sugar until

Note: If duck is bought frozen, remember to defrost the day before use.

yolks are a pale yellow colour and thick enough to ribbon, not drip, when you lift the whisk out of the bowl. Add cognac and beat. Pour the mixture into a small pan and place this pan into a larger one of barely simmering, not boiling, water. Continue to beat for another few minutes until the mixture in the smaller pan becomes hot. Then set the smaller pan over another pan of ice water and beat for a few minutes more with the whisk until the mixture cools again and begins to thicken substantially. Next melt baking chocolate in a heavy saucepan, again over hot water, adding instant coffee, preferably espresso, and stir constantly. Beat into this chocolate the butter to make a smooth, creamy mixture. Then beat the chocolate mixture into the egg yolk and sugar mixture in a large bowl. In another large bowl, and using a clean whisk (essential to remember), beat the egg whites until they form stiff peaks. Now stir a quarter of the egg whites into the chocolate mixture, then fold the remaining whites into the chocolate mixture very, very gently. Spoon the whole mixture, do not pour it, into the ring or charlotte mold, and chill for at least six hours or until it has set firmly. To serve, take a knife and run it around the edges of the mold, set a serving plate upside down on top of the mold and invert the mold very quickly. The mousse should slide out quite easily, but if it doesn't, then repeat the procedure. Just before serving, top with heaping mounds of freshly whipped cream, made simply by beating a pint of whipping cream with one cup of superfine sugar until stiff.

2. *Onion Soup, Caesar Salad:* See Gourmet Menu 7. Prepare while duck cooks.

3. *Duck:* Preheat oven to 500 degrees. Remove the internal organs which should be in a bag in the chest cavity and wash the duck carefully. Dredge the duck with flour. Then salt and pepper duck and place a whole onion in its chest cavity. Wrap the duck in heavy aluminum foil and seal well. Place the duck in a roasting pan in a very hot oven for two and a half hours. In the meantime while the duck cooks, prepare a sauce for the duck by combining the juice of two oranges, the grated rind from the oranges, cinnamon, nutmeg, and dry white wine with cornstarch. Bring this to a boil in a small saucepan on the stove. About fifteen to thirty minutes before the bird is finished, expose the duck in the foil and broil on all sides until golden brown and skin begins to crisp. Take about an ounce of pan drippings from the duck and mix with the orange sauce. Then pour half the orange sauce over the bird and broil a further five minutes on both sides. Mix the second half of the orange sauce with the honey and pour this over the bird. Broil until honey begins to caramelize and bubble. Just before serving cut the joints around the drumsticks so they will be served easily at the table. Then place bird on a large serving platter and carve directly at the table into individual portions. An added touch at the table is to pour some slightly-warmed cognac over the bird and ignite.

4. *Rice:* Boil two quarts of salted water and add the wild rice. Cook for twenty minutes, approximately, or follow the directions on the package of wild rice.

Drain and rinse thoroughly when cooked. Slice mushrooms into thin slices. In a large pan fry the mushrooms in some of the drippings from the cooking duck until well-coated. Then add the rice and a half cup of the same drippings, and Cointreau. Stir frequently and keep covered and hot. Then transfer the rice to a large serving dish and serve with the duck.

5. *Garlic Bread:* Slice an entire loaf of fresh French break thickly, and toast each slice in toaster or oven until golden brown. Remember to keep the slices quite thick. Then prepare a garlic butter by heating butter with cloves of crushed and well-mashed garlic until the mixture is brought to a boil. Skim of the scum that rises to the surface of the hot butter and strain with a small sieve. Then with a basting brush thoroughly coat both sides of all bread slices with the butter and reform the slices into a complete loaf. Loosely cover with foil and put into the still-hot oven, serving hot from oven with rest of the meal in a fancy breadbasket. The bread should be done just ten minutes before the rest of the meal is ready, and should only be in the very hot oven for about five minutes.

****

11 Spanish

Paella
Hot Cinnamon Buns
Sangria

Approximate preparation and cooking time: 3 - 4 hours

Ingredients:

1. Paella*

   1 2-lb. frozen lobster, defrosted
      (or fresh if available)
   6 - 9 large shrimps in their
      shells (fresh if available)
   1 can clams, drained, or 6 - 9
      clams in their shell, fresh
   1 can mussels, drained, or 6 - 9
      fresh in their shells
   ½ lb. smoked pork sausage or
      plain pork sausage
   1 2-lb. chicken, cut into serving
      pieces
   Salt, pepper
   ½ cup olive oil
   2 oz. lean pork, cut into ½-inch
      pieces
   ½ cup chopped onions
   1 tsp. chopped garlic
   1 green or red pepper
   1 large tomato
   3 cups raw white rice
   ¼ tsp. ground saffron
   6 cups boiling water
   ½ cup fresh shelled peas or 1
      8-oz. can peas, drained
   2 lemons

2. Buns

   ½ lb. butter, softened
   1 cup sugar
   1½ cups flour
   6 eggs
   1 tbsp. ground cinnamon
   ½ cup corn or maple syrup
   ½ cup crushed walnuts
   Note: you will need a 12-cup
      muffin tin.

3. Sangria

   ½ lemon
   ½ orange
   ½ apple
   ½ cup superfine sugar
   1 bottle dry red wine,
      preferably Spanish
   2 oz. brandy
   1 large bottle club soda
   ½ lime

Preparation and cooking steps:

1. *Paella:*
   a) With a sharp knife cut away the claws, head, and innards from the
      lobster, but do not remove the shell. Split it in half lengthwise and then
      crosswise into quarters and set the lobster aside. Shell the shrimp, leaving
      the tails, and devein them. Scrub the clam and mussel shells clean if
      bought fresh. If canned, drain and rinse. Set them aside.

b) Cook the sausage in water and slice it into quarter-inch round pieces. Brown the chicken well in the olive oil and put the browned pieces aside. Fry the lobster in a skillet (can be same as one used for chicken), cooking five minutes or until shell begins to turn pink. Brown the sausages in same skillet.

c) Chop the onions, garlic, and tomato (seeds removed) and cut the pepper into strips, also removing seeds and core first.

d) Preheat the oven to 350 degrees about one hour before serving and combine the cooked vegetables, the rice, salt, saffron and the boiling water, in a large ovenproof casserole. On top of the mixture, add the chicken, lobster, sausage, shrimp, clams, and mussels, and sprinkle the peas loosely on everything. Bake uncovered, on a low shelf in the oven for a half hour or until the rice is cooked and tender to taste. Take care not to stir the rice while it cooks. When cooked remove from the oven and let cool for ten minutes. While cooling, cut the lemons into six wedges each. Garnish with the lemons and serve right from the casserole at the table.

2. *Buns:* Beat butter, sugar, and two tablespoons flour until the mixture is well blended. Then beat in eggs. When the batter is smooth, add the remaining flour and the cinnamon and continue beating until smooth. Grease a 12-cup muffin tin and pour the batter into each until almost full. Bake in the oven for ten minutes. Just before serving, about five minutes before buns are done, spoon a mixture of honey and crushed walnuts over each bun and put back into oven for remaining five minutes or until golden brown and honey begins to bubble. Cool and serve.

3. *Sangria:* Cut lemon and orange into quarter-inch slices. Cut apple into thin wedges, first removing the core. Combine the lemon, orange, and apple in a large pitcher with superfine sugar. Pour in the wine and brandy and stir until well mixed. Chill for at least one hour before serving, and when Paella is done and ready to serve, remove Sangria from refrigerator and add one bottle of club soda, stirring again until well mixed. Garnish with slices of lime in each tall glass and serve with plenty of ice.

Note: Ingredients in the Paella can be varied as it suits you, using beef instead of sausage, more shrimp instead of lobster, rabbit or frogs' legs instead of chicken.

****

12 French

Bouillabaise
Corn Bread
Strawberry Crepes
Sparkling Wine

Approximate preparation and cooking time: 4 hours, and a perfect recipe for involving all your guests in preparing.

Ingredients:

1. Bouillabaise

¾ cup olive oil
2 cups onions, thinly sliced
1 cup leeks, thinly sliced
2 lbs. fish heads, bones and trimmings
3 lbs. ripe tomatoes
½ cup fennel seeds (if available)
2 cloves garlic, chopped
1 tsp. thyme
1 sprig parsley or ½ tsp. powdered
1 bay leaf
Salt, pepper
8 cups water
1 cup dry white wine
2 2-lb. lobsters, defrosted, cut up, cracked
1½ lb. each of three kinds white, firm fish
2 lbs. mussels
2 lbs. sea scallops
6 peeled potatoes
1 green pepper
1 lb. peas
2 cups diced celery

2. Bread

1½ cups yellow cornmeal
1 cup flour
⅓ cup sugar
1 tsp. salt
1 tbsp. baking powder
2 eggs
6 tbsp. melted butter
8 tbsp. melted shortening
½ cup milk

3. Crepes

¼ pint milk
¼ pint water
8 oz. flour
3 tbsp. melted butter
1 tbsp. superfine sugar
2 tbsp. cognac or brandy
Cooking oil, preferably peanut
1 pkg. frozen strawberries, defrosted
4 oz. cherry brandy
1 pint whipping cream, or ice cream, optional

Note: You will need one nine-inch pan and one heavy pan or crepe pan.

Preparation and cooking steps:

1. *Bouillabaise:*

a) The court bouillon base: Cook in oil in a heavy saucepan for five minutes, sliced onions, leeks, fish heads, bones, and trimmings, chopped tomatoes, bay leaf, thyme, garlic, salt, pepper, parsley, and fennel seeds. Add the water and dry white wine and cook a further half hour. When cooked strain the mixture through a fine sieve into a large soup pot, taking care to press firmly in order to catch all the juices.

b) Seafood: Cut and crack the lobster and cut all the fish (snapper, halibut, cod, whitefish, haddock, etc.), into two-inch pieces. Wash the mussels and scallops and dry. Set aside.

c) Bring the court bouillon to a boil, add the lobster and boil briskly for five minutes. Then add the fish and cook another five minutes. Finally add the mussels and scallops and cook a further five minutes. Set it at simmer and keep for about two hours at this setting or until fish has all blended into a stew. Add potatoes, cut in rough chunks, one green pepper, likewise cut in chunks and seeded, diced celery, and peas. Cook a further half hour on top of stove and serve with the hot cornbread right at the table, ladling out each portion as desired.

2. *Bread:*
Preheat oven to 400 degrees after Bouillabaise has been cooking one and a quarter hours. Mix cornmeal, flour, sugar, salt, baking powder in a large bowl. Beat, in a separate bowl, a mixture of eggs, melted butter, melted shortening (both cooled first), and milk. Pour this into the cornmeal and flour mixture and beat until smooth. Grease a shallow, nine-inch baking pan and bake the mixture in the preheated oven for a half hour or until golden brown on top and springy to touch. Remove and serve hot in thick slices with Bouillabaise.

3. *Crepes:* Beat milk, water, and flour with melted butter, superfine sugar, and brandy or cognac. When mixture has the consistency of cream, heat a heavy pan brushed with oil and butter mixed together. Pour the batter in, tip it slowly to spread it evenly into a thin sheet, taking care to distribute evenly. Once one side is cooked, usually in a couple of minutes, flip it over very gently with a spatula and cook other side same way. This is tricky, and it will probably take you several tries to get them to turn without tearing. Keep crepes warm once they are cooked by putting them on a plate suspended over a saucepan of boiling water. Then in another small saucepan heat package of thawed strawberries and its juice with cherry brandy until mixture boils. On individual serving plates, place one crepe, open, and spoon the strawberry mixture onto the middle of it. Then turn the crepe, rolling it up until each is in the shape of a roll (much like a jelly roll). Serve each in this fashion, perhaps with some whipping cream or ice cream on top, with coffee for dessert. This could be done at the table in front of your guests, if you have a crepe pan and a stand with a heating element.

Notes

After writing the last chapter, I found that there were so many things left to say that yet another chapter was needed, so here is more.

In a word, this chapter contains more recipes, recipes for everything from soups to desserts. But the narrative style of this chapter represents a decided departure from the menu style used throughout the rest of the book, and I feel I should explain its use.

In my first draft for the first edition, the entire book had been written in this style, recipes included. Then on some expert advice from outside sources, it was decided to change the book's structure to the standard menu style of meal preparation. The book was then supposedly complete. However in an impulsive last minute decision, I decided that I could not part with the recipes that had been eliminated in rewriting the book. So I kept them in narrative style and threw them in as a bonus. They are all easy to prepare, and all will become favourites as you try them. Again, good luck and happy cooking!

More on soups:

Once you have made a basic chicken stock, you are in business for a grand style party recipe from Malaysia called Soto. In making this dish, each guest assembles his soup from a variety of things, all based on a bowl of freshly made chicken stock. What you have to do is provide both the soup and other ingredients. This is not hard to do. What you are really making is a soup buffet.

First take the chicken from the stock you have just made, let it cool, and dice it into bite-sized pieces and pile them into a bowl. Then take some green onions, dice them and throw into another bowl. Next assemble some fried onions (about three will do for six people); a cup of diced celery, leaves and all, in another bowl; and some fried green peppers, taking care not to overcook them, in another bowl. You will need to make some Malaysian rice cubes. Boil some rice, (a cup and a half, uncooked). When cooked scoop it all into a nine-inch square pan, press down hard, and cool thoroughly. Chill it a bit, and then slice it into one-inch squares and pile them into yet another bowl. If you have got some leftover ham, cube it. If you have veal, the same goes. In fact, any leftover meats will do. Then line up your guests and let them serve themselves, buffet-style, creating whatever kind of soup they want.

A great soup to try is Fish, Tomato, and Potato Soup, otherwise known in South America (where it came from), as *Caldillo de Congrio.* To serve eight, you will need 2 tbsp. of olive oil, 2 large onions (chopped), ½ tsp. finely chopped garlic, 6 medium tomatoes (peeled, seeded, and coarsely chopped), ¼ tsp. dried oregano, ½ bay leaf, a tsp. salt, freshly ground pepper, 4 large peeled and diced boiling potatoes, 4 cups cold water, a tsp. fresh coriander, 2 tbsp. fresh chopped parsley, and a 4-pound striped bass, cleaned and cut into one-inch-thick steaks. (You can use any other firm white fish as a substitute.) Cook the onions and garlic until soft but not brown in a large soup pot, add the tomatoes, oregano, bay leaf, salt, and some black pepper, and cook for five minutes. Add potatoes and water, cover and cook for twenty minutes. Then throw in the fish and coriander, cook ten more minutes, and serve.

More on meats and poultry:

Beef

Ground beef must be the most versatile meat in the world, with limitless potential. However, I will talk about only one ground beef dish here, the rest I will leave to others. I assume you know about hamburgers. So I will talk about Chili con Carne, my favourite meal in a hurry and always a delight!

There must be millions of ways to prepare it, but I have relied on this recipe as dependable and tasty. Take 3 pounds of top round, and have it ground fresh or grind it yourself if you have invested in a meat grinder. Cook this in a twelve-inch skillet for three minutes in 4 tbsp. of vegetable oil at high heat, stirring constantly. When it is lightly browned, throw it in a four-quart ovenproof casserole, draining off the fat by using a slotted spoon in transferring it. Cook 2 cups of coarsely chopped onions and 2 tbsp. of finely chopped garlic in 2 tbsp. of oil, stirring frequently for five minutes. Add at least 4 tbsp. of chili powder and a pinch of oregano until the onions are coated. Then, add a 6-ounce can of tomato paste, and 4 cups of beef stock, fresh or canned. Add them to the casserole, throw in some salt and some freshly ground black pepper, bring to a boil, cover the pot, and simmer on low heat for one to one and a half hours. Add a can of kidney beans (about 1½ cups will do nicely), and cook a further fifteen minutes or so. When it is done, it is great!

Next on my list of favourite meat dishes is Boiled Beef with Carrots and Dumplings. Opinion differs here. Someone I know uses short ribs and adds barley towards the middle of cooking. I like that version, but prefer using a 3- to 3½-pound brisket, rolled and tied.

Put the brisket in a four- to six-quart casserole, cover with water, bring to a boil, skim off fat, and simmer at reduced heat for at least two and a half hours. Then, add about 1 pound of onions (small, 10 should do), a dozen small scraped carrots, and some barley if you like, and cook for another three-quarters of an hour. Make the dumplings using 1 cup of flour, ½ tsp. of baking powder, ½ tsp. salt, and 1½ ounces of beef suet (about 3 tbsp.). Mix in a large bowl, working the suet in until the consistency is rough. One-third cup of milk helps bind the mixture, and more will do if it is not binding properly. Shape into one-inch balls.

Drain the meat and vegetables when cooked, and throw the dumplings into the remaining stock. Cook uncovered for at least fifteen minutes, and transfer to the plate of beef and vegetables, kept warm all this time in a 250 degree oven. I then pour the stock over the whole works.

Stews are a welcome addition to any meat menu, and I urge you to become expert at the ones I will give you now. The reason for this is, first, that they are delicious, and second, because they are economical. You can get at least two days out of a well-made stew, and on both days, the stew tastes just as good; you cannot lose.

The first recipe is for a South American beef and vegetable stew with fresh corn, called *Cocido Bogotano.* I suggest fresh corn, but you could use canned corn if seasons limit you. For six to eight people, you will need at least 2 to 3 pounds of boneless stewing beef, preferably chuck, cut into two-inch cubes. (I advise 3 pounds, because as you are making it anyway, you might as well have a bit extra. Remember meat shrinks in cooking, so an extra pound does not finish as an extra pound, it shrinks.) First brown ½ cup of coarsely chopped onions in a three- to four-quart ovenproof casserole in some olive oil for five minutes until they are soft but not brown. Then throw in 2 tomatoes, peeled, seeded and coarsely chopped. Cook for a few minutes and add the meat, a bay leaf, 1 tsp. of cumin, ½ tsp. of oregano, and ¼ tsp. of turmeric, with a chopped garlic clove, some salt, and 6 whole peppercorns. Pour in 3 cups of cold water and a few teaspoons of cider vinegar, reduce heat, cover and simmer for thirty minutes. Add 4 carrots, cut in long slices; 2 to 4 potatoes, cut in chunks; and 4 trimmed celery stalks. Cover and simmer another half hour. Then throw in the corn (4 ears with the husk off, cut into two-inch slices), and some peas (1 pound shelled). Cook again for ten minutes and serve right from the casserole.

Now for something Swedish: Swedish Meatballs. You will need ¾ pound of lean ground beef, ½ pound of ground veal, and ¼ pound of ground pork. Soak bread crumbs (1½ cups fresh, soft bread crumbs) in 1 cup of light cream for five minutes or so. Cook ½ cup of chopped onion in butter until tender but not brown. Mix the crumb mixture, onions, and meat with 1 egg, ½ cup chopped fresh parsley, 1¼ tsp. salt, pinch of ginger, pepper, and nutmeg, until well-blended. Make little balls, about one and one-half-inches each and brown them in some butter. Then make the gravy, using the pan drippings from the meat mixture, some more butter, 2 tbsp. flour, 1 beef boullion cube dissolved in 1¼ cups boiling water, and ½ tsp. of instant coffee powder. Cook, stirring until gravy thickens, and add meatballs. Cover and cook another half-hour, turning meatballs every so often. Serve them either as a main course (there are about thirty meatballs) with rice, or as a side dish if you are energetic and plan to make other things.

Life would not be complete without a recipe for Roast Beef in Wine, so here is one. It is simple to make. All you need is 2 sliced onions, 2 cans of sliced mushrooms, some parsley, 1 can of beef boullion (or your own homemade), and at least 6 ounces of dry red wine. Brown your roast (5- to 6-pound rump), and add the above to it. Season with a bay leaf and a sprinkle of thyme, and cook covered in the oven for a few hours at 325 degrees. Cut and serve in its own sauce. Just like chicken in wine, better known as Coq au Vin, only this once moo'd instead of cluck'd!

What about Hungarian dishes, you ask? Or did you? Well even if you did not I will give you a recipe for Hungarian Goulash; it might come in handy. Make a start with 3 large onions, thinly sliced, 1 tbsp. of cooking oil, 1 tsp. of salt (at least), 1 tsp. of vinegar, and 2 to 4 tsp. of paprika. I suggest 4 but you may find this to be too much. Brown this mixture, then add 2 pounds of boneless beef chuck, cut into one-inch cubes. Brown some more and add 1 cup of dry red wine. Cover tightly and simmer slowly for at least two hours. Add water if necessary during cooking. Serves four to six nicely.

To end the section on meat, I will give you a recipe for using your leftover beef roast, barbecued steak, any leftover cuts of beef you might have. You will need about 1½ pounds of leftover meat. First sauté mushrooms (about 1 pound fresh ones) in a lot of oil (3 tbsp.) with juice from 1 lemon, and 2 tsp. of chicken stock base until mushrooms are tender. Let cool. Slice meat into long shredded strips of about one-half inch wide each. Make a dressing out of 4 tbsp. of olive oil, ¼ cup of red wine, 3 tbsp. of red wine vinegar, a pinch each of chervil, thyme, basil, and marjoram, and the juice left from the mushrooms. Add some salt and pepper to taste. Put the meat strips in a shallow dish and throw the dressing over them. Around the sides of the dish, arrange a nice display of tomato wedges and artichoke hearts, stuffed green olives, and anchovies. Chill for a few hours, basting every so often, and serve. Something different for four to six people.

Chicken

The next set of recipes are chicken recipes, and I love chicken. Some are simple, others more complex. If you do not already love chicken, try some of these and you will flip out over the little creatures.

First, I will tell you how to bone a chicken breast because you will need to know that to make many chicken recipes. To bone a breast cut through the cartilage at the V of the neck. In each hand grasp the small bones on either side of the breast. Bend each side of the breast back, punch up with your fingers to snap out the breast bone. That should do it.

Oriental touches are nice with chicken. Try my Oriental Chicken with Pineapple. You will need eight varying pieces of chicken (whatever you prefer) for this dish. Salt and pepper the meat, and cover it with a mixture of pineapple juice from large can of pineapple chunks, some cooking sherry (6 ounces should do it), a handful of brown sugar, some ginger marmalade, and a sliced onion. Cook uncovered for an hour and a half, then add a green pepper, sliced lengthwise, some sliced water chestnuts, the pineapple chunks, and a handful of bean sprouts. Thicken with cornstarch and simmer until everything is heated right through. Serve on a bed of rice. For a variation on the above, try adding a large container of sweet and sour sauce, bought from your local Chinese food restaurant.

A fast favourite of mine is Chicken in Cream Soup with Rice. Here, you will need 6 drumsticks and 6 wings. Fry them in an electric frying pan in cooking oil, browning them for about thirty minutes at high heat. Then cook the rice separately, using 2 cups of rice. Add 1 can of condensed cream of mushroom soup, 1 can of condensed cream of chicken soup, and 1 can of condensed onion soup (or a package of dry onion soup) to the pan, and let simmer for about forty-five minutes. Blend in rice, heat everything, and serve. Simple and very inexpensive. You can vary the cuts of chicken if you prefer.

Last but not least is a great cold dish, *Escabeche de Gallina*, favoured by the South Americans, and better known to us as cold pickled chicken. To make this, you have to brown 6 to 8 pieces of chicken in an ovenproof casserole on top of the stove. Then add 1 cup of dry white wine, 1 cup of vinegar, 1 cup of hot water, 2 onions cut into wedges, a few carrots cut into thin diagonal slices, 1 leek cut into rounds one-eighth inch thick, some salt, and a bouquet garni made of 1 celery top, 2 parsley sprigs, 2 bay leaves, 2 whole cloves and ½ tsp. of thyme, all wrapped in a cheesecloth bag tied at the end. Bring all of this to a boil and simmer for half an hour. Remove bouquet garni and serve chicken on a platter, pouring the liquid over the chicken. Best to serve this one chilled (at least six hours in the fridge after cooking).

Pork

While not as dear to me as beef and chicken, pork can lend an important variety to your menu. I have selected one recipe that I like using pork.

Double Stuffed Pork Chops is simple to prepare among pork recipes. Buy a half-dozen double loin pork chops (you may have to ask the market butcher for these beforehand). Slash a pocket in the meaty side of each chop and preheat your oven to a moderate 350 degrees. Now you make the stuffing: chop 2 onions and 2 stalks of celery, mixing them with 2 diced apples, skins on or off, 2 tsp. of salt or to taste, some freshly ground pepper, and ½ tsp. of poultry seasoning. Stuff it into the pockets, and bake the chops in a covered baking dish for about an hour and a half. Then take off the cover and bake another half hour until very brown.

Lamb

First the Irish: Irish Stew, what else! Peel 6 potatoes and cut into half-inch squares. Spread half of them on the bottom of a four- to five-quart casserole and cover them with 2 roughly diced onions, and 3 pounds of lean, boneless lamb shoulder (trimmed of all fat and cut into one-inch cubes). Sprinkle with salt, pepper, and thyme, and arrange the rest of the onions (another two, same way) topping with the other half of the potatoes. Add more salt and pepper and some water (enough to cover the whole works). Bring to a boil, then reduce the heat to simmer and cook for about one and a half hours. This is done on top of the stove, but you can do it inside at 350 degrees instead. Serve it right from the casserole.

For you barbecue fans, try Shish Kebab. You will need an 8- to 9-pound leg of lamb, boned, and cut into thick serving pieces or cubes. You also need a basket of cherry tomatoes, and 6 very small onions, 1 pound of small mushrooms cleaned and trimmed, and 4 large green peppers. Cut the peppers into one-inch square chunks. I like to marinate the whole works in a mixture of olive oil, lemon juice, vinegar, dry red wine, garlic (crushed), and onion juice made in the blender from fresh onions, with some cumin seeds and bay leaves thrown in for good measure, keeping it in the fridge for a few hours before using. Skewer the ingredients, alternating everything until you have filled six to eight skewers. Barbecue, basting with the marinade you have left. Try some lamb as you barbecue to test for doneness. Salt to taste and serve informally.

Veal

Only two for you: Osso Buco is first. You will need a shallow, heavy casserole large enough to hold the meat standing snugly in one layer. Then sauté 1½ cups finely chopped onions, ½ cup of chopped carrots, ½ cup finely chopped celery, and 1 tsp. of crushed chopped garlic. Once browned, remove from heat. Take the veal shank (6 to 7 pounds sawed into eight serving pieces and tied with a string around their width), season with salt and pepper, flour, and brown in oil in a heavy twelve-inch skillet. Preheat the oven to 350 degrees, clean skillet, leaving a film of oil, add a cup of dry white wine, and boil until the wine is reduced to half. Then stir in ¾ cup beef stock (your own or bought), ½ tsp. dried basil, ½ tsp. dried thyme, 6 parsley sprigs, 2 bay leaves, and 3 cups of canned whole tomatoes, broken up. Boil and then pour over the veal which is now in the casserole. Bring to a boil on the stove, cover and bake. Keep it in the oven about an hour and a half. Sprinkle with grated Parmesan cheese and serve. Serves six.

The other veal dish is Wiener Schnitzel, better known to most people as breaded veal cutlets. To serve four to six you will need 3 pounds of leg of veal, cut into slices ¼-inch thick. Marinate the meat in lemon juice (1 cup fresh) for one hour. Remove and dry, sprinkling with salt and pepper. Dip in 2 beaten eggs, then in flour, then in 1 cup of bread crumbs. Shake off excess and refrigerate for a half-hour. Heat 1½ cups of lard in a heavy twelve-inch skillet, then add the meat. Cook three to four minutes on each side until brown and serve immediately.

Game

Game is great, but you have to get it first! Not too many people want to slush around in the muck to get these things, so I find the best way is to let someone else get it for you! What I do every year is offer a bounty to my hunting friends. I say, "Tell you what. I will give you a bottle of the best booze of your choice if you bring me back something good from your hunting trip, cleaned and/or plucked. What do you say?" They usually say yes, and in fact most of my hunting friends bring back lots of things for a bottle of firewater! Try it out and see what you can get. Freeze game and it will last at least six months.

If a friend bags a wild turkey, try roasting it at 350 degrees after thorough cleaning, first salting and peppering the insides and filling with a stuffing made with 6 cups of coarsely crumbled cornbread mixed with minced turkey liver, 1½ cups of chopped onion, 1 pound of well-seasoned sausage meat, a pinch of thyme, and ½ cup of cooking sherry. Truss the bird securely, and skewer the cavity shut so the stuffing does not run out. Roast uncovered in the oven for at least two hours, basting frequently with melted butter and pan drippings. Broil the bird (grill setting on your stove) for five to ten minutes until dark brown and serve after letting it cool for ten minutes.

You can cook roast goose in similar fashion, except cooking time is doubled to four hours. To make a great stuffing for this bird, boil 10 potatoes, and partially cook 1 cup of chopped onions, ½ cup of chopped celery, 4 slices of crumbled bread, ¼ pound of ground salt pork, 2 beaten eggs, 2 tsp. of poultry seasoning, and salt and pepper to taste. Rice the potatoes (mash), and add the above ingredients to it. Stuff, and your goose is cooked!

Fish and Shellfish

How about a Seafood Pilaf? Well, why not! Brown ¾ cup of uncooked long-grain rice in butter for about five minutes. Add 3 ounces of broiled sliced mushrooms (easy to prepare); a large can of condensed chicken with rice soup; a large can of crab meat, drained; a medium can of shrimp, drained; ¼ cup of dry white wine; and a cup of minced onions. Place the works in a one and one-half quart casserole, bake uncovered at 350 degrees for almost an hour. Fluff with a fork, and bake a few minutes longer. It serves six nicely.

Now, something from the southern United States: Shrimp Creole. Cook ½ cup of chopped onions, ½ cup of chopped celery, and 1 clove of garlic in some oil and add 1 pound of cooked canned tomatoes, an 8-ounce can of tomato sauce, 1½ tsp. salt, 1 tsp. sugar, a couple of globs of Worcestershire sauce, and some Tabasco sauce. Stir in some cornstarch mixed with water (2 tsps. cornstarch will do) and let thicken. Add 1 pound of shrimp, or a little less, and ½ cup of chopped green pepper. Cover and simmer about five to ten minutes. It serves six, and goes well with curried rice.

A very simple dish to prepare and one that tastes great is Shrimp-Lobster Chowder, made with a mixture of ¼ cup fried chopped celery, 1 ounce onions, 1 large can of cream of shrimp soup, 1 large can of cream of mushroom soup, 1 soup can of milk, 1 cup of light cream, 4 ounces of fresh shrimp, a 5-ounce can of lobster, 1 tbsp. of fresh parsley, and ¼ cup of dry sherry. Mix, cook on top of the stove and finish in the oven, broiling for a few minutes under a grating of Parmesan cheese.

Late at night you may want to prepare a Shrimp Quiche for your friends. For this you will need 10 ounces of fresh or frozen peeled, deveined, diced shrimp; ¼ tsp. of Worcestershire sauce; a squirt of Tabasco sauce; a half-dozen unbaked pastry tart shells; a few eggs; 1 cup of light cream; ½ tsp. of prepared mustard; 1 tbsp. of flour; ½ tsp. salt; 4 ounces each of shredded Swiss and Gruyère cheese. Mix the cheese and flour together, and mix the other ingredients together with some salt and pepper. Line the pastry with the cheese mixture, then add the shrimp mixture. Bake at 400 dgrees for a half-hour or so and serve. You can feed six a nice light snack this way, topping it off with a light dry white wine.

Brook trout is a nice fish to prepare, either fresh or from the freezer. One per person is perfect. Sprinkle them with salt and pepper inside and out. Then dip into 2 cups cornmeal, and cook in bacon fat for about five minutes each side. Serve hot with crisp bacon strips (one per fish).

Lobster Newburg is elegance personified. It is an easily prepared dish that will serve six or eight comfortably. Cut up 3 cooked fresh lobsters, or three 8-ounce cans. Brown in a large skillet in butter for about a minute. Pour in ⅓ cup of dry sherry and 1 cup of heavy cream, and bring to a boil. Reduce heat and simmer for a couple of minutes. Then beat 5 egg yolks into ½ cup of cream and add 4 tbsp. of simmering lobster sauce, pouring all of this back into the skillet slowly. Cook over moderate heat, taking care not to bring to a boil. Season with ¾ tsp. salt, ⅛ tsp. cayenne pepper, ½ tsp. of lemon juice, and serve immediately on a bed of steaming rice. A final touch is a sprinkle of paprika on top for effect. Elegant!

The recipe I am going to close this section with is refreshing anytime. To make Pickled Tuna Salad open a can of tuna, drain and break into pieces in a bowl. In another bowl, blend ½ cup of white wine vinegar, ½ chopped onion, ¼ tsp. dill seed, 1 bay leaf, a pinch of allspice, ¼ tsp. of dry mustard, ½ cup of sliced celery, and 1 sliced tomato. Pour this mixture over the tuna, and put it in the fridge overnight. Just before serving add ¼ cup of mayonnaise, mix and spoon onto 6 lettuce leaves. Top with anchovies.

More on desserts

Most of the desserts I am going to talk about are quite simple and middle of the road when it comes to richness. After all, if you are like me, and tend to watch your weight, you do not need to know how to make really fattening desserts, do you?

A very simple pie to bake, and one that tastes delicious, is Chess Pie. It is an old Southern recipe. For it, you will need to mix 2 cups of sugar and 1 heaping tbsp. of flour together and add ½ pound of butter, blending until it is all light and fluffy. Then, add 6 eggs, one at a time, beating after each is plunked in. Add ½ tsp. of vanilla and 2 tsp. of grated lemon peel, put into an unbaked pie shell, and bake at 300 degrees for a little over an hour. Serve it topped with jam, jelly, or preserves.

The above recipe called for an unbaked pie shell; so I think now is the time to give you the recipe for one. A friend gave me a great and dependable recipe. Take 5 cups of flour and combine them with 1 tsp. of salt, 3 tbsp. of white sugar, 1 tsp. of baking powder. Cream one pound lard with a fork and blend together with the dry ingredients. Then crack 2 eggs in a measuring cup, add 1 tbsp. of vinegar and fill the cup to 1 cup with ice cold water. Pour this into the dry mixture, work until mixed, and knead the dough (the more kneading the better). Makes enough crust for about three or four pies and can be frozen in foil.

Here is another pie to fill the shells. To make Apple Pie, peel 8 tart apples, slice very thinly, and sprinkle with 1½ tbsp. of fresh lemon juice. Combine 1 cup of sugar, 1 tbsp. of flour, ½ tsp. of nutmeg, ½ tsp. cinnamon, and mix with the apples. Let the apples stand overnight. Then heap them into a nine-inch pie shell, with the juice made from the apples sitting overnight, and toss on a little butter all over. Top with a pie crust, fluting the edges to seal the whole thing. Brush crust with melted butter and sprinkle with sugar. Bake in a 450 degree oven for ten minutes. Then reduce the heat to 350 degrees and bake another forty-five minutes. (I like mine slightly overcooked.) Serves about six hungry dessert eaters.

Everybody loves Strawberry Shortcake, especially in the summer; so here is a simple recipe for small ones. Mix 4 cups of flour, 6 tbsp. of sugar, 5 tbsp. of baking powder, and 2 tsp. of salt together in a large mixing bowl. Add ½ pound of butter or margarine, and rub together with your fingers until it all resembles coarse meal. Pour in 1½ cups of heavy cream, and mix until you have a soft dough. Throw the dough onto a floured board, knead it for a minute or so, then roll out into a circle, cutting out 6 three-inch circles and 6 two and a half inch circles, and bake them on a lightly buttered cookie sheet for about fifteen minutes until golden. In the meantime, chop a pint of fresh, very ripe strawberries coarsely. When circles are done spread them on the bottom circles, sprinkle with a good measure of sugar, top with fresh whipping cream, and then top with the smaller circles. Garnish with another pint of fresh strawberries, dividing the berries equally among the cakes, and top with a dab of whipping cream.

Cheesecake is a favourite with me. One simple recipe is as follows: Beat 24 ounces of cream cheese with the yolks of a half-dozen eggs until smooth, and then beat into this 1 cup of sugar, 2 tbsp. of flour, 1 cup of sour cream, and 1 tbsp. of both fresh lemon juice and vanilla. Whip the egg whites until stiff, then fold into the mixture. Pour into baked pie shell and let cool. Then chill for a couple of hours before serving. It makes a simple but delicious cheesecake.

What about the times you feel hungry for something sweet but you do not want to go out and buy all those gooey buns at the market? Try making Tea Scones and serve them still warm with freshly-made whipping cream and some jam or preserves. Easy to prepare, and ever so tasty when you want something sweet and filling, but not too sweet and filling! Preheat your oven to 400 degrees, and grease a large baking sheet. In a large bowl, combine 1 tbsp. of sugar, 2½ cups of self-rising flour, ½ tsp. of salt, and 3 tbsp. of chilled lard, cut into tiny pieces. Rub together by hand until it resembles coarse meal, and beat 1 egg until it froths. Set aside 1 tbsp. of the egg and beat ½ cup of milk into the remaining egg. Pour this over the flour mixture, and toss the works with your hands until you can make a ball out of it all. Roll it out on a floured board until three-quarters of an inch thick and, with the rim of a glass, cut into two-inch rounds. Bake for fifteen minutes until golden and serve warm, with jam or preserves in the middle, and whipping cream on top.

Crepes are a versatile dish. (See Gourmet Menu No. 12.) One can fill them with almost anything. Try jams, jellies, or sweet cottage cheese. Put them in a moderate oven until golden brown. Top with a sauce made with brandy and sugar, honey and cognac, or maple syrup. I suggest making a large cheese-bacon-ham-and-egg omelette, and rolling a portion of the omelette inside each crepe, closing with a toothpick through the middle, coating the whole thing with butter, and browning in the oven. Topped with maple syrup and whipped cream, this is about the best breakfast-in-one I have ever had! Jewish people prefer another version, where cottage cheese is mixed with sour cream and sugar, and the crepe is rolled up and cooked in butter for a few minutes. When done, it is served with sour cream on top while still hot. These Blinzes are fabulous for Sunday brunches, and you should try them.

Notes

Index